Character Formation and
Identity in Adolescence

CHARACTER FORMATION AND IDENTITY IN ADOLESCENCE

Clinical and Developmental Issues

Randolph L. Lucente
Loyola University Chicago

LYCEUM
BOOKS, INC.
Chicago, IL

© Lyceum Books, Inc., 2012

Published by

LYCEUM BOOKS, INC.
5758 S. Blackstone Ave.
Chicago, Illinois 60637
773+643-1903 (Fax)
773+643-1902 (Phone)
lyceum@lyceumbooks.com
http://www.lyceumbooks.com

Cover image © Roman 1963—Dreamstime.com

6 5 4 3 2 1   12 13 14 15

ISBN 978-1-933478-69-2

Printed in the United States of America.

Library of Congress Cataloging-in-Publication Data

Lucente, Randolph L.
  Character formation and identity in adolescence : clinical and developmental issues / Randolph L. Lucente.
    p. cm.
  Includes bibliographical references and index.
  ISBN 978-1-933478-69-2 (pbk. : alk. paper)
  1. Personality development. 2. Personality in adolescence. 3. Character. 4. Identity (Psychology) 5. Adolescence. I. Title.
  BF724.3.P4L83   2012
  155.5'1825—dc22

                                                              2011016033

To Meredith and Elizabeth,
and to my patients and my students

Contents

Acknowledgments

The author gratefully acknowledges permission to reprint portions of the following material with the kind permission of Springer Science and Business Media:

Lucente, R. L. (1986). Self-transcending and the adolescent ego ideal. *Child and Adolescent Social Work Journal*, *3*(2), 161–76.

Lucente, R. L. (1988). Adolescent dual unity: Identification and differentiation in development and treatment. *Child and Adolescent Social Work Journal*, *5*(3), 157–70.

Lucente, R. L. (1996). Sexual identity: Conflict and confusion in a male adolescent. *Child and Adolescent Social Work Journal*, *13*(2), 94–114.

The author gratefully acknowledges permission to reprint portions of the following material with the kind permission of Routledge, Taylor & Francis Group:

Lucente, R. L. (1987). N=1: Intensive case study methodology reconsidered. *Journal of Teaching in Social Work*, *1*(2), 49–64.

Lucente, R. L. (2008). Affectivity: Regulation, identity formation, and metaphorical thought. *Psychoanalytic Social Work*, *15*(1), 1–27.

Lucente, R. L. (2009). Mentalizing in the therapeutic relationship with an older adolescent: The case of Fred. *Psychoanalytic Social Work*, *16*(2), 87–99.

Preface

The writing of this book was prompted by many considerations and is the result of over thirty years of teaching, research, and clinical experience with adolescents and their families. In fact, my very first exposure to practice with adolescent clients derived from my initial field internship in the MSW degree program at the University of Illinois at Chicago in 1971, and my interest in this fascinating clinical population has never waned. It is my belief that a depth-oriented approach to practice will of necessity involve the integration of the adolescent developmental stage with theories that provide an understanding of normality and pathology and with the practice tools that will enable the clinician to be effective as an informed treatment provider. The book is therefore illustrative of the fit of theory with practice and elucidates the pivotal concepts of traditional psychodynamic theory. These core concepts (for example, from ego and self psychology and from attachment and object relations theory) have over time undergone significant revisions, and it is my intent that a postmodern, contemporary treatment of this literature will serve to inform the current changes taking place in both practice and knowledge developments, especially vis-à-vis neuropsychobiology.

The book showcases the treatment of adolescent clients through the use of extended clinical vignettes from some of my previously published works and thus represents a synthesis of theory and practice that has paralleled my faculty appointment in a school of social work best known for its clinical mission at the master's and doctoral levels. These clinical vignettes highlight the interplay of clinical process and developmental theory. They explore the evolving construction of identity in the adolescent stage, the formation and organization of character, the processes of a second separation-individuation, and the capacity for affect regulation and the related self-reflective function that are the prelude for adult experience in all subsequent phases of the life cycle. These vignettes feature an intersubjective approach to practice, examining such clinical phenomena as engagement, working through, choice of intervention, resistance, transference, and countertransference. The adolescent clients, the subjects of these case studies, presented with disorders on the borderline/narcissistic spectrum, ones that clinicians frequently encounter in practice, for example, identity confusion, character deficits, and the acting out of intrapsychic conflicts that suggest arrests in development in the early processes of object relating and attachment. The narrow focus of this work, on intensive, individual psychotherapy, clearly differentiates it from other texts on adolescent clients which typically cover a much wider spectrum of client dysfunction and describe a variety of other practice modalities such as family systems, brief treatment, or cognitive behavior therapy. These texts are panoramic whereas mine is clearly more selective and depth-oriented.

The text has a characteristic organization that consists of an initial review and integration of theory that is followed by a detailed clinical analysis of a psychotherapy. Chapter 1 introduces the reader to the core elements of the text and its theory bases: identity, the ego ideal, character formation, and the clinical process. Chapter 2 focuses on the structure of the self from traditional ego psychology points of view—Freud, Blos, and Erikson—as well as from self psychology. The clinical study identifies the adolescent's dysfunctional narcissism, relative to the grandiose self and idealized parental imago pole, and how the treatment relationship was able to reach and eventually resolve these psychodynamic conflicts. Chapter 3 reviews attachment theory and object relations—attunements, internalized working models of the mind, and fixations in symbiosis and separation-individuation. Two case studies illustrate the working through of splits in self and object representations characteristic of separation pathology. The fourth chapter presents an integration of traditional object relations theory with the current research on affect development, including data from neurobiology. I treated the adolescent clients, a fourteen-year-old male and an eighteen-year-old female, in long-term insight-oriented psychotherapies that were intersubjective, mentalizing, and self-reflective. The book ends with a chapter that attends to the strengths of case methodology and to the characteristics of clinicians as reliable and valid data collection instruments as they immerse themselves in the therapeutic process with mindfulness and an attitude of an evenly suspended attention.

Adolescent Development and Clinical Process

The focus of this book is the development of character in the adolescent stage, with its larger context being identity formation and the various component structures that make up its totality, and the interrelated processes of a second separation-individuation. Because of the broad utility of a psychodynamic approach to both development and psychotherapy with the adolescent client, each chapter is fueled by theories that inform complex, biopsychosocial assessment, diagnosis, treatment planning, and choice of interventions. These psychodynamic theories reflect the points of view afforded by psychoanalysis, ego, domain, and self psychology, and attachment and object relations theories. As the contemporary and evolving postmodern philosophy of science in the clinical realm has been impacted by research data from infant developmental studies and findings from neuropsychobiology, these rich knowledge sources that inform the treatment relationship, that is, the inherent intersubjectivity of the uniquely configured, subjective worlds of therapist and client, will be applied to the discussions of the clinical material that follow in each of the subsequent chapters. There will be no attempt to dilute the intrinsic complexity of concepts derived from these psychodynamic theory and research sources; rather, the intent will be to present them in a coherent, understandable, and hopefully integrative manner to facilitate their use by clinicians who practice with this challenging age group.

The themes of the book illustrate the interplay of theory and practice. The dominant motifs are the multiple, psychodynamic points of view that contribute to an understanding of adolescent character development, personality pathology *in statu nascendi*, and symptom formation, and thus provide a perspective on the continuum of what is normative and what is dysfunctional. The focus is both developmental and clinical, and the client vignettes that follow illustrate the treatment issues that all clinicians face and the skills sets required for engagement, developing the treatment relationship, initiating and maintaining the

1

therapeutic alliance, using the transference/countertransference relational continuum to good advantage, and therapist judgments that inform the choice of interventions. These extended clinical vignettes provide an entree into the worlds of adolescent clients diagnosed with a number of complex and multifaceted disorders, broadly including the borderline/narcissistic spectrum and the identity confusion that is frequently seen in all teens who have experienced arrest in earlier developmental stages: psychosexual, psychosocial, attachment, separation-individuation, and self development. Symptoms of conflict, the acting out of dysfunctional character patterns and trends, pathology of the self, and defenses—how they ally to prevent coherent narratives and serve to interfere with affect regulation and identity integration, autonoesis, and reality orientation, and so on—all are the subject matter of these clinical explorations.

Subsequent chapters elucidate the pivotal concepts of traditional theory. These classical theories include object relations (e.g., M. Mahler and D. W. Winnicott), self psychology (e.g., H. Kohut, M. Basch, and D. N. Stern), attachment theory (e.g., M. Main and P. Fonagy et al.), and ego psychology (e.g., E. H. Erikson, P. Blos, and G. Rose). The core concepts of these theories have continually informed both research and practice since their earliest formulations. However, with the changes currently taking place in knowledge development, it is the book's purpose to present a contemporary, postmodern perspective by integrating psychoneurobiology data into the psychodynamic orientation to practice, clarifying and elaborating the clinical and the theoretical dimensions in the two areas of concern, that is, identity and character formation.

Identity

Betwixt and between childhood and adulthood, the adolescent stage for all theorists has been viewed as a stage of consolidation and the eventual stability of functions. Blos (1962) has observed that the late stage adolescent possesses (1) a highly idiosyncratic but stable arrangement of ego functions; (2) an extension of the conflict-free ego sphere with increased secondary autonomy; (3) an irreversible sexual orientation; and (4) stable mental apparatuses. "On the way to consolidating identity" for the late stage adolescent (Lucente, 1996, 2008) involves (1) an adultomorphic body image rooted in one's core gender as unambiguously male or female (Stoller, 1968); (2) mature psychosexual drive organization, that is, genitality, and a sexuality that expresses itself via arousal for a preferred erotic object (S. Freud, 1905b, 1923, 1924; Erikson, 1959); (3) autonomous, independent functioning, that is, a second separation-individuation with capacities for object and self constancy (Mahler, Pine, & Bergman, 1975; Blos, 1962); (4) moral reasoning utilizing hypothetico-deductive thought and internalized ego ideals (Kohlberg, 1976; Gilligan, 1993); (5) a mature narcissism reflective of the goals, ideals, and ambitions that have been divested of their infantile, grandiose, and omnipotent valences (Kohut, 1971); (6) an evolved, superordinate ego-superego system, that is, an executive apparatus that organizes the various components of the personality (Blanck & Blanck, 1974, 1986); and (7) a maturing capacity for affect regulation and related processes, for example, autonoesis, mindsight, and empathy (D. J. Siegel, 1999, 2007; A. N. Schore, 2003; Fonagy, Gergely, Jurist, & Target, 2002; Allen, Fonagy, & Bateman, 2008).

A sense of identity begins in early infancy as the undifferentiated matrix gradually becomes, paradoxically, a dual unity through symbiotic fusion of infant self with maternal object (Mahler et al., 1975). With minor variations between theorists and researchers, for example, Hartmann (1939), Spitz (1965), Winnicott (1960b), Bowlby (1969), Klein (1932, 1935), and Sander (1980), the process describes a shared merging of ego boundaries wherein maternal supplies are equated, perceptually, with the infant's needs of the moment for food, comfort, and soothing. This dual unity results from the infant's search in the first months of life for an attachment, a hypercathexis of the maternal object as an internalized representation, first experienced narcissistically as an omnipotent part of the self in a highly complex affective field (Emde, 1980). This pinnacle achievement of oneness from attachment, a dual unity, becomes the basis for progressive, autonomous development through all successive epigenetic stages and amounts to a *primary identification* through the mechanism of incorporation. The ensuing primary identification with the mother establishes the body ego of the infant as a libidinized object for the infant's very own observation and use. In addition, the infant gains a sense of basic trust (Erikson, 1963) that the world will forever contain the necessary supplies needed for further growth and development. Finally, primary identification serves a progressive function, not only in his object relationship with the mother, but also in the entire outer world experiencing of basic reality.

The epigenetic sequence leading to, but not including, the consolidation of identity in the adolescent stage contains four pivotal reference points, each bearing on the internalization of enduring personality traits that shape the adolescent's performance in all areas of functioning preparatory for adult roles. This psychosocial package through the first six years includes being a trustworthy object for others, a capacity for autonomous activity without undue loss of self-esteem in interdependent relations, and a purposeful pursuit of libidinally tinged relationships with the opposite sex coupled with appropriately competitive, yet deferential, relations with same-gendered peers and older authority figures, alike (Erikson, 1963). These first six years of childhood expand on Freud's epigenetic model of psychosexuality à la the oral, anal, and phallic-oedipal erogenous zones and their internalizations as part objects, identity points, in the context of an overall body ego (S. Freud, 1905b, 1923). On the cusp of preadolescence, the latency male and female at the age of twelve have acquired a repertoire of skills and aptitudes suggesting potential competence in the sex-appropriate behaviors prescribed by one's culture and agency in their future enactments of the adult sexual role. By the end of adolescence proper, the teen has integrated all formative identifications into a stable, adult-to-be configuration that is a unique blend of innate constitutional givens, the vicissitudes of aggressive and libidinal object relations, special aptitudes and talents, and the opportunities afforded by social roles (Erikson, 1963).

A core task in the adolescent phase is erecting an adult-to-be sexual self concept. The term *sexual identity* is fraught with a variety of meanings and implications, and the noun form, *sex,* has a multitude of denotations in the English language. The word *sex* can variously mean an anatomical classification (male or female), an act of intercourse, or membership in a group of individuals with similar characteristics neither necessarily, nor even primarily, having to do with the genitals. In considering its adjectival form, particularly when a prefix has been appended to it, the word takes on even more ambiguous connotations. To be heterosexual, bisexual, asexual, or homosexual all convey a sense of specific and typical behaviors, none of which are mutually exclusive, related to sexual acts as well as to relationship attachments in a larger, but ill-defined, interpersonal context. Few other words evoke as much human curiosity and interest—or share the same level of uncertainty and ambiguity.

Sex assignment for males and females is decisively fixed at the point of conception by the simple presence of the Y chromosome on a strand of DNA. While biologically determined and genetically immutable as male or female in morphology, masculinity, femininity, and sexual identity, on the other hand, are all socially constructed and the products of the considerable variabilities afforded by constitution, further development, the vicissitudes of interpersonal experience, and culture. Thus, attitudes, beliefs, convictions, and personal characteristics shape how an individual expresses maleness and femaleness, relative to a personal sexual identity, through an internal code of related behaviors and external choices of erotic objects. And the process is not fixed but instead remains fluid for many—both male and female sexuality may take many forms over the remainder of the adult life cycle. However, extrafamilial erotic expression assumes its pivotal, seminal stamp in adolescence.

Gender differences in sexual identity for the male and female adolescent are most salient relative to the genitalia. From birth the infant male is anatomically different from the infant female. The male's primary maternal identification, as an object relations representation of his mother, simultaneously contains elements of self-differentiation based on his penile anatomy. In the symbiotic orbit of fused part-self and maternal part-object experience (Mahler et al., 1975), differences are retained that equate the anatomical similarity of son and father side by side with the dissimilarities of mother and son. Likewise, the anatomical similarity of mother and daughter facilitates a more encompassing primary identification as the enduring identification with her mother represents sameness. For the male, however, the enduring identification of son with mother contains a body self-representation that distinctively signifies his separateness rather than similarity. For the son, his mother's qualities of femaleness serve as the prototype for future erotic object finding, rather than for identification, whereas the counterpart infant–mother experience for the female, leading to her primary maternal identification, fosters congruence rather than separation. In the overall context of individuation, the task for the male of de-identifying with the mother is conditioned by the physiological similarity of son and father. Current theories on gender differences suggest that the daughter's maternal identification in the symbiotic phase is more enduring, more encompassing, and longer-lasting than the male's (Gilligan, 1982; Jordan, Kaplan, Miller, Stives, & Surrey, 1991; Chodorow, 1989). Because her primary identification never shifts, the femininity of the daughter may be more firmly established and more secure, therefore, than is masculinity in the male (Stoller, 1968). Finally, elaborating further on these polarities of closeness and distance, intimacy, enmeshment and isolation, the relationship needs and interpersonal styles of the male will likely be characterized by themes of autonomy and individuation, whereas attachment and differentiation themes will more typically become the modus operandi for the female. In this fashion separation-individuation processes for the male and female, while universal, configure somewhat differently for the two genders, and these differences will be evident in the internalizations that eventually congeal into a stable sense of identity at the end of the adolescent stage.

With a focus on self-concept, self-esteem, and competence, Harter's extensive research on multidimensional emotional thought describes how the adolescent male and female develop increasingly complex, cognitive representational sets for the processing of the categorical affects (Harter & Buddin, 1987). At the most basic level (1.0, age five), young children are unable to integrate two different feeling states simultaneously (e.g., anger and sadness) to the same target, a sibling. However, by the end of the latency stage, most preteens have a conceptualization of how multiple emotions interact within a variety of interpersonal contexts at the same time. With a fluid shift in perspective and focus the same individual at the age of twelve years (level 4) can reflect on both positive and negative affects attached to the same or different targets and then coordinate these affective meanings into a coherent narrative. This research continues to explore the affect regulation function in the developing adolescent self as cognitive-emotional, social, and interpersonal processes. These representations—the internalizations of self and other and the construction of emotional states that in particular derive from relationships—continue to further modify and expand the cerebral neural networks involving D. J. Siegel's eighth sense of attunements and attachments (2007).

The development of the self in relationships with peers and the self representations which the young adolescent internalizes are viewed as interactional between processes that are cognitive, affective, and social (Harter, 1999). The rudiments of these self representations directly involve experiences with parents, other adult authority figures, and peers and an awareness of the distress states associated with the emotions of shame, envy, embarrassment, and humiliation and the pride based on personal accomplishment and approval from others. To the extent that the latency-age child has a perceived sense of self-worth, from an inner correspondence of competence and successful agency and from an external match of respect and unconditional positive regard, the stage will be set for an adolescent passage that will either be discordant with the sense of self or integrative. For Harter, all children have experienced the affects of shame, embarrassment, and pride but for those with an enduring, stable self-esteem it is the latter emotion that will prevail.

The passage from the end of latency through adolescence is parallel for the genders but only in regard to preparing, in general, for their respective future roles and responsibilities. The transition for female adolescents is decidedly more complex than for the male in a patriarchal culture where the hallmarks for maturity consist of self-sufficiency, autonomous functioning, and adherence to moral rules where justice is defined as "doing the right thing" and making the "right choices" based on universal, abstract ethical principles and constructing model relationships with others in an "affect-free" public forum. Described as a "loss of" or "lowered voice" (Gilligan, 1993), a crisis of connection (L. M. Brown & Gilligan, 1992) or as a "self in relations" (Jordan, 1997), a vast literature on the psychological perils facing female adolescents has emerged to vividly portray the challenges to retaining her sense of the centrality of her personal commitment to relationships with others rather than adopting a false self that reflects cultural prescriptions for the construction of her feminine identity—being passive, dependent, nurturant, immaculately hygienic, self-sacrificing, and not too bright.

For the female adolescent, connectedness, empathy, and mutuality remain the central features of the mother–daughter experience in her transition to womanhood. Her primary identification with her, therefore, solidifies a sense of self and confirms at the same time an inner voice that relationships, reciprocal intimacies, and enduring commitments to others constitute the most important realities of living. This relational self is also validated in her peer relations as attachment dynamics are replicated in a second separation-differentiation that is modeled on the first. As she matures with enhanced capacities for self-reflection and the narration of a personal attachment history, however, this inner voice, one which is congruent with her true self and her core, must face the crisis of a culture's sex role expectation that she devalue these very same qualities of nurturance, affect expressiveness, and preparedness to mother that define her identity (Chodorow, 1989). When positioned to make a heterosexual commitment to a man, her early oedipal history will also likely contribute to this crisis of connection as the exclusivity that she once experienced with her father is unlikely to be thematic of her intimacy with her partner. Other postmodern revisions of the relational experiences of male and female adolescents can be found in the research and theory that continue to deconstruct linear, binary, and traditional stage-related models of psychological development. An example would be the Boy Code (Pollack, 2000) that imposes on males an expectation of being tough and hyper-independent, controlling feelings and keeping them private, projecting a superhuman image of physical strength, and above all else of "being cool"; this only serves to alienate youth and estrange them from their inner experience.

The concrete dilemma for the oedipal child of five is the fact that there exist only two genders. On the other hand, the dilemma for the adolescent male and female in search of a congruent sexual identity to operationalize with peers, in the second oedipal undertaking, is the variety of erotic object choices afforded each of them. Money (1974) has pointed out that, at birth, each individual has two basic templates that govern sexual orientation. One pertains to expressing erotic behavior in same-gendered relationships and another for opposite-gendered relationships. And there exists a multiplicity of partial influences that help determine each of these strivings as well as serving to elaborate their inherent complexity. These influences are cultural, hormonal, constitutional, environmental, and chromosomal. The permutations on the themes of heterosexuality, homosexuality, bisexuality, asexuality, and autoerotic sexuality are confounding to adolescents with identity confusion (Reiter, 1989; T. Sullivan & Schneider, 1987; Stoller, 1968). This inherent duality of identifications and object choices is but another variation on the theme of the innate bisexuality to which Freud (1924) referred as operant in adult psychosexuality. Kestenberg (1980) has suggested, too, that in addition to the psychobiological template of a universal bisexual predisposition, there exists hormonal evidence of male androgens and female estrogen present, simultaneously, in the bloodstreams of each gender. All of these factors are dramatically featured, clinically, when a young adult with a history of gender confusion, cross-dressing, and an adolescent identity disorder requests hormone therapy and sex reassignment surgery at a sexual dysfunction clinic (Becker & Kavoussi, 1988).

The epigenetic model of libidinal drive development, and the attainment of genital primacy in late adolescence, have been formulated exclusively from a psychoanalytic, psychodynamic theory base. Throughout the adolescent subphases, the sexual drive is decisively modulated as it becomes increasingly attached to the primary and secondary sexual characteristics of the changing genitalia in the pubertal female and male (S. Freud, 1905b; Blos, 1962). Libidinal interests that were once pre-oedipal—oral and anal modalities—undergo a change in function and become organized around an enduring, sexual body-self representation that is anatomically intact and adultomorphic in form and function. This process serves to anchor the primary attributes of each gender's reproductive function, which are anatomically fixed and objective, that is, sex = male = phallic and sex = female = vaginal, around the much more elusive qualities of maleness and femaleness and the attendant gender role expectations of one's culture, which are variable and subjective.

In the early adolescent phase, genital masturbation accompanied by erotic, pleasurable fantasies with or without orgasm unite to loosen pre-oedipal psychosexual fixations and reaffirm a non-castrated body self-image (for the male) and an intact sexual body self-image (for the female). Masturbation in early adolescence, that is, Blos's preadolescent regression and the early adolescent subphases, fuels the fantasies of bisexuality for each of the genders, with the attendant tasks of initiating a second separation-individuation and resolving the negative oedipal complex. While a precondition for the attainment of an unconflicted heterosexual identity in the adolescence proper subphase—as masculine versus merely male and as feminine versus merely female—the sexual body self-representation is further enhanced by one's self-definition as masculine or feminine in outlook, object finding, code of behavior, and in mirroring confirmation through the eyes of male and female others alike. When guided by a central masturbation fantasy that is heterosexually based (Laufer, 1968), the stage is set for entry into relationships that confirm one's masculine and one's female heterosexuality. While autoerotic and narcissistic, masturbation is the pathway for sexual expression that resolves any lingering residues of bisexual conflict. Of course, confirmation of intact maleness and femaleness as the core gender attributes will have to await actual erotic experiences in adolescence proper.

Thus, falling in love with intimacy, romance, and sexual passion highlighted by the words "I love you" solidifies one's sexual identity as does no other experience. No adult ever forgets their first adolescent love. Genitality is confirmed relative to organ mode, code of conduct involving loyalty to a significant other, and masculine and feminine behaviors. What is inner and congruent corresponds to the sameness perceived by an affirming object. In this passionate relationship with a female peer, the male carries out an identification with his mother as well and object images that are feminine and ego alien are modified through the re-internalization of traits that become affiliated with the self (Schafer, 1968). Nurturance, expressiveness, affectivity, dependency strivings, and tenderness are integrated into one's masculine sexuality via a line of development in love relationships that repeats core elements from the first intimacy in infancy with the mother. For the female adolescent, what is ego alien—male morphology and masculine gender characteristics—is simply assigned to the male partner as his sole, rightful province through projective identification, in this fashion both replicating and validating elements of her relationship with her father. The relationship, therefore, between anatomical certainty and maleness and femaleness in the larger contexts of sexual identity is reciprocal and not linear.

In summary, the core identifications for the five-year-old male and female oedipal child were those with the parents, of the same gender, that will have provided a stable foundation for all of the future *secondary identifications* that will further elaborate and differentiate their identity structures toward the end of the adolescent stage and throughout adulthood. These secondary identifications become divested of castration anxiety, bisexual conflict, projected or displaced aggression, and jealousy from the first oedipal stage and thus reflect a more individualized and autonomous identity complexity. Having evolved past their original conflicts associated with the aggressive and libidinal drives of the first phallic-oedipal phase—no longer serving the function of defense—these secondary identifications become ego syntonic and promote secondary autonomy and mastery in the conflict-free ego sphere (Hartmann, 1939; Rapaport, 1951, 1958).

Other aspects of identification that influence the overall construction of identity in adolescents include *identification with the aggressor*. For instance, a ten-year-old on Halloween awakes from a frightening dream in which she is being attacked by a goblin. Early the next morning, donning her Halloween costume, she awakens her younger sibling from sleep, scaring her as she reverses roles from passive victim to active aggressor. Later that morning the same daughter, unaware that she harbors jealous feelings toward her sibling, the "baby of the family" because she is treated as "daddy's favorite" and receives preferential treatment from both parents, gives her the last three pancakes on her plate at breakfast even though she is still hungry herself. In this fashion, the older daughter *identifies through altruistic surrender* (A. Freud, 1946), participating as if she is a loving parent, and basks in the praise that comes from her selfless act as she vicariously enjoys her sister's pancake meal that was once to be her own. Implicit in this morning replay are the aggressive and libidinal drive components that are evident in both of these mechanisms of identification with the aggressor and identification through altruistic surrender. While they also partake of some degree of denial, undoing, and repression, it is significant that both mechanisms are primarily object-bound defenses with important elements of self and object internalizations. As to repression, by day's end the elder sister has probably forgotten her dream. As to denial, her solicitous behavior with her younger sibling serves to disguise the underlying conflictual, jealous affects. Similarly, her superego prohibition against aggression hides her sense of guilt and, aligned with the undoing defense, rewards her for the masochistic sacrifice, the donation of her pancake breakfast to her sister.

Splitting and *projective identification*, in particular, possess a special significance throughout all of the adolescent substages. The latter mechanism will come to mediate much of the relationship dynamics toward the end of the adolescent phase, and all adolescents normatively utilize both mechanisms in their relationships with significant others, family members, and peers alike through all of the second separation-individuation stage that will eventually establish their independence and autonomy as young adults-to-be. Projective identification, as a more advanced form of primitive splitting, involves interpersonal reenactments, that is, displacements of early conflicts from the first separation experiences of toddlerhood, wherein part self and part object representations, and their associated affect states, are projected onto others, as repetition compulsions, to replicate unresolved psychic trauma involving introjections. These current interpersonal reenactments for the adolescent frequently involve role reversals with aggressive, affirming, or rejecting part selves and bad part objects.

Blos provided us with an extended case narrative that amply illustrated the multifaceted dynamics in the treatment of a twelve-year-old's use of projective identification defenses in her transference relationship with her therapist (1970). Abandoned and exiled to a distant midwestern state to live for a year with her aunt and uncle at the age of five, Susan's second individuation in early adolescence featured regressive trends to the original trauma. Many months into the middle phase of her four-year-long psychotherapy, and argumentatively stating that treatment was ineffective and deriding her therapist as a skunk and a stinker, she announced that she would be terminating at the end of the hour, never to return to the office. Her threat to break off treatment in the present re-created her earlier experience of rejection by her mother (the bad part object) as she turned from a passive position as abandoned victim to active agent in initiating the breakup; after all, "leaving is easier than being left behind" (REM, 2004). That Susan never missed a single appointment over a four-year therapy attests to the power of projective identification mechanisms as potently object bound. These repetition compulsion dynamics included her internalized representation as a good self in interaction with a bad part object.

In addition to becoming an executive in attempting to master her original separation trauma, she affirmed herself by offering to give one-half of her therapy
hour to the little boy whose appointment preceded hers and half an hour to the
adult male who came after her. Her treatment thus contained many themes of
a double gender identity confusion as she pondered out loud if she were a boy
or a girl, and the self-sacrificing donation of her treatment hour to the two
males amply demonstrates her identification through altruistic surrender as she
offers to relinquish the treasured relationship with her therapist.

Because all of the identification mechanisms remain object bound as they
serve relational needs relative to significant others, each one contributes to the
structure of the ego in its object relations function. Elaborating and maintaining
interpersonal experiences over time, each one contributes to the development of
a unique identity. As the "character of the ego is a precipitate of abandoned object cathexes" (S. Freud, 1923, p. 15), these object relations elements empower
the ego as an integrator in the tripartite model of the mind as it becomes increasingly dominant as a regulator of internal tensions, emanating from the pressure
of the drives for immediate discharge and from the demands of the impinging
environment, the external world of reality.

Proposing a different way to conceptualize identity, Winnicott located the
core of identity in the experiences of the true self and in the structure of an adaptive false self that permits the expression of the true self without excessive interference or control from the demands of the outer environment (1950, 1958,
1960a). These two selves, the true self and the false self, are not binary constructions; they blend into one another and therefore share a permeable membrane
that permits each self to influence the other. Expanding his formulation to include a third area of self structure between the true self and the false self (1963),
he described an intermediate area that was pleasurable, explicitly communicated, and simultaneously congruent with the inner needs of the individual and
the outer demands of the environment.

While the transitional process and the creation of an intermediate area of
experience relate to the interpersonal construction of infant–mother reality
(Winnicott, 1951), it is in the formation of the true self, however, that the infant
constructs what is most personal, prized, and private. The true self relates to the
construction of what is inside and intrapsychic. This "inside," as differentiated
from the world of intermediate experience and knowledge of external others,

comprises the core of the central, or true self. It consists of a sense of continuity of being, a personal psychic reality, and a personal body scheme (1960a). It is a function of the holding environment to protect and to isolate the true self from environmental impingements by operationalizing transformations of primary maternal preoccupation into good enough mothering. While similar to the defining elements of the core self of interpersonal theory, for example, self-agency, self-coherence, and self-history (D. N. Stern, 1985), the Winnicottian formulation of true self structure lacks the former's exclusive interpersonal focus: to flourish and grow, the true self must be permitted its privacy.

The relationship between innate aggression and the development of the true self is primary rather than ancillary. Spontaneous id expressions of rage and opposition to a frustrating environment serve to define one's inner personality core by establishing external boundaries and further differentiating the true self from the other internalized selves. It is the maternal empathic attitude that initially facilitates the formation of the true self by permitting the infant to indulge normal grandiosity, aggress actively, and pursue pleasure lustfully. The ultimate guarantee of a viable true self, however, is the erection of a false self to defend it. Therefore, in light of its guardian role, the corollary false self is every bit as important a self structure as the true self. Their relationship is reciprocal and each requires the other. As the infant complies with the mother's needs at the expense of his own, the false self gradually becomes "society syntonic" by presenting a socially acceptable façade of intellectualizations and culturally prescribed reaction formations to hide from outer view the internal core of his real experience, real emotion, and real self-identity (Winnicott, 1950).

The concepts of isolated and parallel play (Erikson, 1963) augment this theory of true self-development. The maternal holding environment that fosters personal discovery provides intersubjective experiences of being alone while still in the mother's presence. This capacity to function alone, yet to remain connected intrapsychically, is the hallmark of true autonomy (Winnicott, 1958). To play in her presence under the illusion of being separate is to create and modify her object representation in fantasy. This actually strengthens the infant's tie to reality. The aggressive use of the maternal object in fantasy promotes a sense of a shared interpersonal reality that can stand the test of the infant's destructive omnipotence. Structurally, as a result of these intense interpersonal and intrapsychic processes, the self-system evolves to incorporate a protected and esteemed true self, an identification with a valued real other, and a capacity for real relationships that exist and flourish despite projective-introjective phenomena.

The Ego Ideal

Nearly every author whose topic has been adolescent psychological growth underscores the centrality of the fluctuations of ideals, idealizations, values, and moral judgments as the domain of this stage. Though uniformity among theorists of adolescence exists in the importance placed on ethical matters, there is considerable disagreement over the explanations for these changes. The psychoanalytic explanation for changes in the morality of the adolescent hinges on the upsurge of the drives that reawakens long-repressed oedipal constellations (positive and negative), the successful resolution of which marks a change from primitive to mature superego structure (S. Freud, 1917; Novey, 1955; Schafer, 1967; Hartmann & Lowenstein, 1962; Loewald, 1980b; Jacobson, 1971). Other explanations include the psychosocial maturation of the adolescent and the achievement of an evolved ego identity (versus identity diffusion) that is experienced as integrated and constant from within and as stable and definable by others from without (Erikson, 1963, 1968). A third view traces the evolution of values and ethics on the basis of the adolescent's ability to make moral judgments that involves decentering (Piaget, 1965; Nass, 1966; Edelson, 1978), the capacity for abstract reflective thought that characterizes the period of formal operations (Piaget, 1950; Kohlberg, 1976), and movement beyond an egocentric role towards empathy for, and altruistic behavior toward, another (Aronfreed, 1970; Staub, 1975; Selman, 1971; Kohut, 1971). Clearly, when it comes to morality, moral reasoning, and an underpinning moral structure, the literature abounds with conceptualizations, all of them having significance for better comprehension of the universal ethical throes of adolescents.

What appears to be missing from much of this literature, however, is the relationship between the universal regression of the early adolescent and the later unfolding of his capacity for a more autonomous set of values. Such a relationship has been demonstrated to exist, clinically, in case studies (Blos, 1970) and has been asserted to be a natural progression in the maturation of the child's ego ideal.

> This ideal ego . . . gradually becomes an ego-ideal . . . seen in a much
> more differentiated and elaborated form than previously in parental

figures . . . The future state of the ego (ideal) is to be attained by merging with the magical object. No stable internal structure representative of the ego's self-transcending exists as yet; *the self-transcending is dependent on a magical communion with an ideal authority* . . . taking an intermediate position between external and internal. (Loewald, 1980b, 47, emphasis added)

Freud conceptualized the ego ideal as a personal ego structure when he first discussed it in his early paper on narcissism (1914). In that formulation, the subject treats his own ego (body) as a beloved object, this enhancement representing a libidinal hypercathexis or love of self. The body ego model, derived from the story of the Greek youth Narcissus who fell in love with his reflected image in a pool and drowned as a consequence, is a very personal one and lends weight to the view that Freud intended the ego ideal to be tied to the structure of the self and to secondary narcissism in particular. A second important development in this essay was the author's statement that the ego ideal is a substitute for the lost narcissism of childhood, that is, for the belief that one's parents are omnipotent and that the child will therefore share in their perfection, protection, and power. Throughout the essay, Freud describes the ego ideal in noteworthy, personal terms that clearly differentiate his writings on the subject of the conscience, or superego, which instead utilize notions of prohibition, inexorable law, societal sanction, and punishment by higher authority. Third, Freud noted that idealization and sublimation go hand in hand, that both processes share similarities in that each is goal-directed and frequently interpersonal, involving the rerouting and transformation of primitive libido into more complex channels, that is, the behaviors that promote adaptation and self-respect. Finally, the ego ideal can perform a personal censoring role, serving as watchdog over latent dream contents that might otherwise overwhelm the less than conscious awareness of the dreamer and interrupt his sleep.

In an attempt to include the ego ideal in the larger context of the individual's representational world, Sandler, Holder, and Meers (1963) posited the formation of an ideal self, arising from the introjective processes of childhood whereby clusters of self representations, as distinct from object representations, coalesce into a self-I-want-to-be. From another theoretical stance, Kohut (1971) describes the developing child's idealized parental imago which forms the basis for these more mature, later transmutations of narcissism into values, ethics, and ideal strivings. A final stamp in late adolescence seals this process, as a unique identity emerges that contains one's idealizations and a self concept in alignment with one's object choices and identifications (Jacobson, 1964). Such a developmental model would locate the ego ideal within the larger context of an ego identity, itself made up of internalizations composed of self and object representations. The ego ideal would be subject to the function of reality testing, thereby providing a linkage to the topography of mental activity, that is, to unconscious, preconscious, and perception-conscious modes (Sandler et al., 1963; Erikson, 1968).

The ego's role in the structural entity, the functioning ego ideal, would be to review and assess the matrix of all self-representations and the corresponding affects, attributes, cognitions, images (object representations), and memories tied to them. A synthetic function would emerge here as well. The resultant adolescent ego ideal would be, therefore, an aspect of one's ego identity, function in the ego sphere of the tripartite model and "could be said to represent a set of to-be-striven-for but forever not-quite-attainable ideal goals for the self" (Erikson, 1968, 210).

Character Formation

The psychoanalytic literature on character formation in adolescence has been relatively sparse for the past two decades; however, prior contributions—particularly those of Erikson and Blos—continue to inform this area of interest. Both authors note that character traits can be identified in children long before the adolescent passage, but the sum total of these character traits does not, in linear fashion, simply add up to character organization. Thus, the achievement of a stable character organization becomes another one of the central tasks of the adolescent stage. This organization, with its stamp at the end of the stage, represents a character synthesis that defines in myriad ways how the adolescent displays predictable and typical, albeit unique, attitudes, interests, and habitual responses to dilemmas involving interpersonal relations and the pursuit of goals.

From the classical literature (S. Freud, 1913, 1931; Blos, 1968) character traits are linked to specific levels of drive development, for example, the oral fixation which promotes dependency strivings in the anaclitic mode or the anal fixation which fosters compulsive styles and the attendant obsessions. This same literature describes the defensive aspects of character traits which serve to ward off anxiety. Finally, Erikson's formulation of character attended to the influences of culture, the social environment, and history. All of these early contributions suggest that character emerges from conflict, the "economic gain" of character traits is the expansion of one's adaptive potentials, and character traits replace repression with reaction formations that relieve the experience of signal anxiety having undergone a change of function (Hartmann, 1939). In this fashion, character organization is an integrative process and serves a regulatory function by containing discordant, conflictual affect states, thereby stabilizing the ego and aiding it in maintaining its homeostasis. One's character is, to a significant degree, equated with significant aspects of one's self: "one feels at home in one's character" and for some, "one dies for it before letting it die" (Blos, 1968, p. 260).

The endemic ambivalence and splitting mechanisms that dominate so much of the adolescent's psychic life show up as binary "polarities" (Blos, 1962, pp. 73–74), ones that shape the behavior, attitudes, wishes, and fears, and which mediate interpersonal relationships. These polarities have conscious and unconscious components and reflect the active and passive expression of the defenses, especially the reaction formations that attend to being rebellious versus being submissive, the acceptance of others versus their rejection, idealism versus materialism, asceticism versus self-indulgence, altruism versus egoism, loyalty versus faithlessness, being outgoing versus being introverted, and pity versus callousness. These fleeting, ever-shifting attitudes can all be observed in early adolescence and signify that true character organization has yet to be achieved and is undergoing revision prior to stability. To the extent that these polarities dominate the character structure of adults, an arrest in the adolescent stage has most assuredly transpired.

For Freud, the character of the ego is a precipitate of abandoned object cathexes (1923) whereas for Erikson, identity as structure begins where identification as defense ends (1968). The psychosocial, epigenetic timetable posits eight core tasks from cradle to grave, and universally each stage of development has an expectable crisis, a timeline for the mastery of the central task, that is, a proper rate of ascendancy and decline, and potential for arrest or fixation due to unresolved, unfinished business (Erikson, 1963). It is noteworthy that Erikson's stages of trust versus mistrust, autonomy versus shame and doubt, and initiative versus guilt all involve the internalizations of basic elements of character. To be trustworthy implies that one keeps promises, is a man of his word, does not deceive others, and is "true blue" and loyal. These are basic character traits that establish and define an individual as a reliable object for others. Having been amply provided for in a nurturing holding environment that resulted in a primary identification with the maternal object, one becomes a potential source of libidinal supplies for others.

In regard to the next three stages and in similar fashion, to be autonomous suggests exerting one's will and possessing fortitude in the face of adversity; in short, one is a "self-starter," does not "waffle" under pressure, and does not experience undue shame and embarrassment. Displaying initiative versus guilt implies that an individual possesses drive and ambition, does not easily retreat when the "going gets tough," and has leadership abilities versus being compliant or subservient to domineering others. In the fourth stage, industry versus inferiority, the focus for mastery refers to the facile use of the tools of one's culture—educational success in the classroom with the three Rs and the computer. This stage involves the various roles, as well, in peer culture activities, for example, capacities for being a leader as well as a follower of others. All of these stages of psychosocial development witness internalizations, that is, representations of the self in interaction with objects, and each one has themes that are central to the formation of character traits in the child that will eventual consolidate at the end of adolescence.

The most notable neo-Freudian contribution to the study of character formation comes from Karen Horney (1945), whose interpersonal theory of psychoanalysis linked three relational patterns—moving toward, against, and away from people—to three related basic conflicts. Horney's compliant character type, those "who move toward people," similar to the oral character described by Freud, seek security in dependent relations. Their goal is to never be alone, and the love of compliant characters for others is possessively selfish. Repressed aggression is a significant factor in all of their interpersonal activities. Those character types "who move against people" aggressively exploit, manipulate, and dominate others, and their goal is to compete and win, "doing unto others before they do unto you." In the extreme, such individuals possess asocial and amoral personality trends. Their antisocial behaviors predominate in their interpersonal styles where life is viewed as a survival of the fittest. Horney's third character type, those "who move away from people," are detached and secretive. While not necessarily shy, they are estranged from others and prefer their own company. Exuding an independent lifestyle, any sign of reliance on others is perceived as a major shortcoming and a sign of weakness. In the extreme, such individuals display schizoid characteristics and their motto, to paraphrase Polonius's advice to Hamlet, is "to thine own self be . . . enough." The "moving away from people" character types have replaced real relationships with imaginary ones because true intimacy with a partner would present a threat to their core self. For all of Horney's character types, the core conflicts involve a dysfunctional mix of motives, fears, wishes, attitudes, and expectations that are repetitive, rigid, and all-consuming. In the extreme, these basic conflicts inhibit the individual's potential for flexible problem solving and prevent mastery of conflicts in pursuit of growth and purposeful change.

The character traits that will come to frame and define a personality system at the end of adolescence have significant cognitive, behavioral, and affective features. Character traits include repetitive, interpersonal patterns of interacting with, relating to, and communicating with others. These traits are observable in all people and are usually devoid of conscious conflict or anxiety; therefore, the individual typically experiences his character traits as ego syntonic. While character traits serve many masters, including adaptive as well as defensive solutions to needs and conflicts, most were mobilized early in childhood to cope with the internal pressures from the drives—the wishes and fears attendant to aggression and sexual impulses—and interpersonal demands from significant others in the familial environment that would include impingements from the personality deficits of caretakers.

All individuals possess character traits, and for most they represent the perfectly normal individual differences that contribute to an interesting, heterogeneous mix of people in all of their variegated splendor in a family, organization, or community. Examples of character traits run the gamut from compliant, polite, self-effacing behaviors in a pacifistic, non-combative personality to the adversarial intrusiveness of an aggressive defense attorney who badgers the prosecution's witness with a suspicious cross-examination that implies his obvious guilt regardless of how he answers the questions. Other examples include overreliance on others, stubborn defiance, intrusiveness, belligerence, embarrassment, perfectionism, stinginess, chronic tardiness or chronic promptness, perseverating, temporizing, conscientiousness, exhibitionism, flirtatiousness, contempt, and exploitiveness. And the list goes on.

When character traits become obligatory, rigidly engrained, and maladaptive, they prevent mastery of conflict and interfere with the maintaining and deepening of relationships with others. At this point the diagnosis of a personality pathology may be permissible. The three cluster personality disorders section of the *Diagnostic and Statistical Manual of Mental Disorders* (*DSM IV-TR;* American Psychiatric Association, 2000) for nosological codings on Axis II has specifications for ten separate categories of diagnosis: paranoid, schizoid, schizotypal, antisocial, borderline, narcissistic, histrionic, avoidant, dependent, and obsessive-compulsive. The criteria sets for each diagnostic entity include enduring patterns of inner experience and inflexibility, traceable to childhood or adolescence, that consist of typical interpersonal behaviors, related cognitive styles, and characteristic attitudes as well as orientation to external reality. However, because the adolescent stage is one of flux and change, as character traits await consolidation prior to entry into young adulthood, no definitive diagnosis of a character disorder prior to the age of eighteen is advisable; rather, a tentative statement of "trends," "organization," or predominant defenses should be rendered on Axis II, for example, borderline personality organization, narcissistic, asocial trends with acting out, splitting, and denial.

Intersubjectivity and Adolescent Psychotherapy

The initial phase of treatment with the adolescent client starts with the first contacts and ends with an agreement to continue, that is, the treatment contract. The intermediate goals of this first phase include (1) getting to know the patient as a person who is distinct from the symptoms that have propelled him into therapy; (2) the rendering of two diagnoses, a nosological classification as well as a psychodynamic statement of the clinical issues, recommending either supportive or insight-oriented procedures or both, after extensive examination of the presenting problem in all of its contexts, within the patient's current biopsychosocial surround and vis-à-vis the past history; (3) recognizing early forms of resistance and attending to them strategically; (4) awareness of the meaning of cultural difference if it applies to the dyad; (5) using trial interpretations, irrespective of the diagnosis, to gauge the capacity for self-observation and insight; (6) if a previous therapy has any "loose ends," resolving them and moving on to forge a new relationship; (7) instillation of hope and encouragement to continue; and (8) clarifying the nature of confidentiality and the limits to privileged communication.

There are a number of viable approaches to guide the collection of the data necessary for evaluation and for rendering a diagnosis of adolescent psychopathology. These include the *DSM IV-TR* (American Psychiatric Association, 2000), which is a prototype and symptom cluster approach; the axes of the expanded *Psychodynamic Diagnostic Manual* (PDM Task Force, 2006), which incorporates findings from neurobiology and the attachment research literature; Brandell's psychodynamic model that lists eight distinct components of assessment covering regulatory personality structures, for example, affects, ego functions, and the self system (2004); and the model from Meeks and Bernet (2001), which reflects the biopsychosocial point of view. The most frequently used diagnostic system for adolescent conditions, that proposed by Meeks and Bernet, directs attention to six arenas for assessment. The first involves the role of constitution and the extent to which psychopathology may be related to biochemistry or an inherited familial pattern (e.g., a bipolar disorder). The second arena for investigation relates to the highest level of psychological development attained and potentials for regression to arrests or fixation points—a carefully conducted history may establish unmastered tasks from the oral, anal, or phallic phases or trauma, for instance, in the processes of attachment or separation-individuation. The third arena for inquiry formulates the most characteristic mode of object relating—is the adolescent primarily shy, withdrawing, narcissistic and manipulative, dependent, inappropriately intrusive, paranoid, or rebellious? Fourth, why does the adolescent appear to be disturbed now? It may be that he has been conflicted for a very long time with an underlying, waxing and waning anaclitic depression but only now has decompensated as a result of a rejection by a romantic partner. The fifth arena questions the extent to which the adolescent displays a sense of being distressed or conflicted. Are the symptoms of dysfunction experienced as ego alien or as ego syntonic? If they are of the latter valence, considerable pressure from the family or referral system may be necessary to deal with the initial resistance to treatment. Finally, if the adolescent enters treatment, will the family be able to comply with the recommendation and accept the implications for supporting the changes the adolescent will be making in her life? Incorporating all six elements of the Meeks and Bernet schedule, MacKenzie (2007) has expanded the original with four additional arenas for evaluation. First, are the adolescent's defenses primarily mature or immature, adaptive and sublimating or maladaptive with projection, acting out, or denial everywhere in evidence? Second, what is the nature of the family system? Third, are there significant areas of diversity (ethnicity, race, spirituality, oppression, socioeconomic status, or culture) that heavily influence the adolescent's psychosocial surround? Finally, what is the availability and nature of the resources, both internal and external, that speak to the resilience or vulnerability of the adolescent to stress and crisis?

Irrespective of the evaluation and assessment system chosen to guide the diagnostic process, the pivotal issue is that the biopsychosocial assessment should be inclusive, comprehensive, and multifaceted in the organization of the data involving observation, clarification, and the use of nomenclature. The underlying principle in a psychodynamic formulation of conflict is that most symptoms of psychological dysfunction are profoundly overdetermined in their etiology and expression rather than unitary or static. It is for these reasons that a developmental structural orientation is recommended to guide the clinician in all aspects of the diagnostic and assessment phase. The developmental structural classification system first described by Greenspan and Polk (1980) provides a conceptual framework for locating personality functioning on a spectrum that ranges from fully adaptive to grossly pathological. This approach is etiological and begins with a search for an identifiable antecedent causal agent that precedes the effect, that is, the outcome or occurrence of a mental dysfunction. At the same time it is also structural because it considers the individual's capacities, for example ego functions, self system, superego integrity, affect regulation, and internalized attachment working models in stage-appropriate terms. Clusters of symptoms with behavioral, cognitive, affective, and interpersonal features are all tied, therefore, to the current life stage with expected levels of personality organization deriving from previous stages of development. Finally, the developmental structural classification scheme orders the severity of impairments from those that are most to those that are least severe: (1) defects in ego functions (e.g., loss of reality testing, incoherence, or disintegration anxiety); (2) major constrictions in personality functioning (e.g., splitting of self and object representations, severe character pathology, or incohesive self structure); (3) encapsulated disorders (e.g., symptom and character neuroses); and (4) intact, flexible functioning (e.g., occasional, episodic symptomatic reactions to phase-appropriate stresses).

Numerous texts on adolescent treatment exist in the literature, and most describe the first phase as one of engagement that will eventually establish the therapeutic alliance, the mutually shared "fund of trust" (Basch, 1980, p. 133) and partnership, which encompasses the entire treatment relationship including the transference and countertransference elements, the working through of conflicts in the middle phase, and the termination decision. Studied and researched for decades, the literature on psychotherapy outcomes has consistently demonstrated that establishing and maintaining the therapeutic alliance correlates significantly with client improvement (Lawson & Brossart, 2003; Frieswyk et al.,

1986; Luborsky et al., 1980; Marziali, Mamar, & Krupnick, 1981; Horvath & Symonds, 1991; Martin, Garske, & Davis, 2000). A more detailed review of the initial phase of treatment and the role of the therapeutic alliance can be found in Lucente and Mishne (2010).

The cardinal rule from the first contacts with the client to engagement is to painstakingly pursue the presenting problem in all of its variations as completely as possible. This extensive focus on the presenting problem has purpose because the internalized core of conflicts and their multiple meanings will emerge with greater clarity only at a much later stage in the treatment. Because these intrapsychic conflicts are camouflaged in this initial phase, elaborating on the presenting problem in the beginning will permit a much fuller comprehension and working through of the underlying dynamics as they pervade all aspects of the client's life space and functioning.

The vast literature on psychotherapy at the level of interventions, in general, has addressed two broad classifications of technique: supportive psychotherapy and insight-oriented psychotherapy. Supportive techniques—ones that primarily stabilize, maintain, and soothe—attempt to keep current functioning optimal and prevent further regression (Lucente & Mishne, 2010). These techniques include universalization, whereby clients are helped to feel that their responses, emotionally, are typically what others would feel under similar circumstances, thus sharing a similarity to the rest of humankind rather than feeling isolated or disconnected. Other interventions include observation of the person-environment fit, clarification, exploration of the psychosocial surround, posing alternative constructions, subtle suggestion, and offering advice. These supportive measures focus on understanding and dealing with current emotions and exploring interpersonal relationships with family, friends, and authority figures. Effectively operationalized, these supportive procedures enable the patient to keep "an even keel," enhancing the use of mature defenses such as sublimation and humor that possess adaptive value, and lessening the use of primitive mechanisms, for example, projection and denial, that tend to be self-defeating in the long run. Described as "here and now" interventions, supportive techniques attempt to reduce distortions of self-experience, promote reality-oriented appraisals of others' behaviors, and minimize black-and-white, all good/all bad concrete thinking. The instillation of confidence that therapy will be of benefit, with albeit hard-won rewards, and encouragement to continue also have their place in the supportive treatment arsenal.

The goals of an insight-oriented psychotherapy are more far-reaching and ambitious than those in supportive treatment. Focusing on the interior mental and emotional life of the client, and dealing with representations of internalized experience that reside primarily in the unconscious, the goal is to make these underlying conflicts conscious (Lucente & Mishne, 2010). The hallmark of an insight-oriented approach to the patient's conflicts is the use of interpretation through which the client experiences the same mental representation in two separate regions of the mind at the same time: the conscious memory of the therapist's words and the unconscious memory, in symbolic or condensed form, of a feeling, fear, wish, attitude, experience, thought, or event. The closer this content is to consciousness, or rather the ease with which it may be moved to the preconscious and beyond the repression barrier and censor to awareness, the less likely it will be subject to resistance and returned to the dynamic unconscious (S. Freud, 1923). Over time interpretations provide connections (1) from the present to the past and to represented inner experience and (2) from the unconscious to the preconscious-conscious system. Interpretive activity, fostering insight and increased capacities for self-observation, is contingent on the therapist's capacity for empathy and the ability to regress with the client's clinical material through an attitude of evenly suspended attention (S. Freud, 1912b). The bi-personal, relational field—a therapist/client "mutually shared unconscious" (Lyons-Ruth, 1999)—is the forum that permits the clinician to come to some kind of understanding based on deduction, induction, or an intuitive hunch triggered by a clinically valid, subjective fact (Ogden, 1994) which he then shares with his client as an interpretation.

The distinctions between insight-oriented and supportive psychotherapy can be frequently blurred, and in actual practice both sets of interventions are utilized. For instance, it would be likely that a successful, two-year-long insight-oriented psychotherapy had included significant preparatory work with supportive procedures predominating. And the corollary is also valid—effective supportive work over time should produce some degree of insight into the nature of a client's inner conflicts.

The central feature of the crucial, middle phase of treatment is the working through of intrapsychic conflicts, arrests in development, and internalized maladaptive patterns of relating. Informed by an intersubjectivist orientation, the clinician provides an experience-near opportunity for the adolescent to reflect on, understand, adjust, and eventually to regulate emotion. Unconscious implicit patterns of relating from infancy and childhood gradually emerge in the treatment relationship as primary emotional experience (D. Brown, 1993; Lucente, 2008) and serve as the forum for the activation of therapeutic empathy. Revisiting the separation-individuation phase for a second time, the adolescent client in a "two person-shared unconscious" dialogue (Lyons-Ruth, 1999) with the clinician addresses these early areas of arrest and conflict, permitting their repair in the middle phase of treatment.

Gabbard (2005) has identified three mechanisms or modes of client change in this middle phase of treatment. First, through interpretation the client achieves insight into the inner experience of fears, fantasies, wishes, attitudes, and interpersonal experiences which include transference phenomena and characteristic relational patterns. In particular, interpretations of defense, when successfully operationalized, promote self-awareness and expand the client's range of attention both internally as well as to external reality. As less of lived experience requires a mobilization of defensive solutions, the membrane of the repression barrier itself becomes more flexible and semi-permeable. This maximizes the potential of the client system to become increasingly complex and multifaceted in its relations with the environment and with represented inner experience. Second, the therapeutic relationship itself, beyond technique, readily lends itself to an enduring identification with the clinician. Having found himself in the therapist's mind, these implicit experiences of "feeling felt" (D. J. Siegel, 1999) gradually permit the adolescent client to expand his self-narrative, incorporating these new elements of a narrative self into a more coherent identity that becomes increasingly more explicit and consciously self-observing. This new knowledge of the client as a self, discoveries derived from the clinician's intensive focus on his patient's inner experience, is the unique product of a psychodynamically informed psychotherapy.

Finally, there is the therapeutic activation of the relationship dynamics in the transference itself, ones that replicate in displaced form the first attachment process with caretakers. The mentalizing, reflecting, and related mindsight features of the therapist in dialogue with his adolescent client set into motion a change process in the cerebral networks and encodings the adolescent brought with him to the treatment. Therapy unfolds as an emotional experience for both contributors in the dyad to their unique therapeutic culture, and this newly created illusory orbit in between self and other revisits the first holding environment. The brain's affect centers, those that regulate so much of human experience in so many different domains of experience, engage with a potential for facilitating significant structural change to the cerebral circuitry.

The integration potential for the adolescent client is multifold and hemispheric. Structural integration can occur both within the hemispheres as well as between the hemispheres in the bilateral but asymmetric brain. This integration potential is maximized through interactions that are also between two minds, ones that are mediated by communication processes at all levels of mentation, through the verbal flow of speech in explicit narrative dialogues and through a nonverbal resonance that encodes implicitly and affectively (Trevarthen, 1993, 1996). Therapeutic attunement operates to create maximum cohesion within the left hemisphere as the adolescent's linguistic constructions assume an ever-increasing complexity involving word choice, nuance of meaning, and logic. Relative to the mentalizing, autonoetic, and self-reflecting functions localized in the orbito frontal cerebral cortex in the right hemisphere, therapeutic attunement promotes greater facility in recognizing emotions, attending to them, and linking them to elements of the client's autobiographical past, present, and future. This form of integration is vertical and top/down, from the orbito frontal regions to the amygdala and brain stem. Both hemispheres—the right as analogic, metaphoric, and context-dependent and the left as biased to logic, language, and linear causality—develop greater flexibility and complexity as separate structures.

The most important and enduring integration, however, is bilateral, that is, between the two hemispheres. Bilateral integration is achieved as the relationship dyad bridges two minds as well as their four hemispheres. The result is an enhanced narrative identity that is informed by cognition and contextualized with affect. The role of the hippocampus in narrative construction is central to identity formation. Because of its structure—it is equally distributed in the right hemisphere as well as in the left—and because of its location next to the amygdale, its multiple neural pathways afford a continuity of cross-talk, bilaterally, between the two hemispheres (Cozolino, 2002; D. J. Siegel, 2007). The early development of the hippocampus in the third year involved linguistics, narratives of self in interaction with caretakers that were encoded verbally and primarily in the left hemisphere. This relationship to linguistics and autonoesis, which is a function informed by the affect centers beginning with the amygdale, never changes and can become increasingly complex as these neural networks become primed through repeated use. Because the hippocampus continues to develop well into adolescence and beyond into adulthood, with an ongoing myelinization of its neural pathways, narrative revision through psychotherapy always remains a distinct possibility.

Without formally addressing its integrative functions, Freud's papers on technique, particularly those explicating the role of interpretation, foreshadowed the intersubjectivist understanding of the mechanisms of client change, the therapeutic action of the treatment relationship to bring about improvement. Freud's attitude of an evenly suspended attention (1912b), isomorphic to the patient's "free associations," permits the therapist to relate to clinical material by self-observing, introspecting, and resonating. This would include his own mentalizing of self experience through mental time travel into his own psychodynamic past history. That these personal insights into his intrapsychic life are juxtaposed to the client's free associations in the here and now assures that a vertical integration is occurring within two unconscious minds. The interpretations that may arise from this form of therapeutic reverie that connect the two unconscious minds, however, are all encased in words. Thus, the linguistic renderings are in turn mediated in the conscious minds dialoguing with one another through the medium of speech. Topographically, in the system unconscious, preconscious-conscious, the words as presentations cross the repression barrier above it and below it (S. Freud, 1915a, 1915c), and to the extent that they have altered the original imprints, these representations and their meanings (after all, words are symbols) account for their new integration. This is the therapeutic action through technique in an intersubjectivist, mutually shared interchange. Neurobiologically, these two systems, one that is actively unconscious and the other that is actively preconscious-conscious, correlate with mental processes occurring in the right hemisphere, the former, and with mental processes occurring in the left hemisphere, the latter (Cozolino, 2002). In this fashion, integration is achieved as the language-based, logical, and digital Freudian secondary process modes of thought connect with the affective, metaphoric, somato-sensory, and id-dominated Freudian primary process modes of thought (A. N. Schore, 2003).

That the "talking cure" requires a verbal dialogue is a tautology; that the stage of adolescence witnesses a transformation into cognitive complexity from the concrete operations of the latency years to advanced, hypothetico-deductive reasoning processes is a universal phenomenon known to all developmentalists. What is now understood with insights from neurobiology is that this transformation from concrete to formal operations and abstract reflective thought cannot occur without what Piaget has referred to as "nutriment" (1950, 1965), that is, a two-mind psychology of interpersonal connections and social relationships with others as opposed to a psychology solely of the individual. In the therapy dyad, the matching of the two left hemispheres which specialize in searching for cause-effect explanations, deducing linear relationships between variables, and in the use of language to assign meanings to events, ensures that the adolescent client's cognitive equipment will be fully engaged in a hemispheric workout of his intellectual musculature. This form of hemispheric integration is vertical as the lower functions of the left hemisphere, for example, the encodings of first words and narrative from the third year, connect with the neocortex that is undergoing a stage-specific revision to abstract reflective thought.

Narcissism, Character Formation, and Separation-Individuation

Narcissism and Ideals: Ego Psychology

In two of Rapaport's most elegant discussions of the structure, function, and operations of the ego, the eminent ego psychologist described the ego's twin fundamental autonomies, (1) an inherent autonomy from stimuli arising from an internal state of drive tensions which originate within the id, and (2) an inherent autonomy from the demands of an impinging environment emanating from without (1951, 1958). While both sets of autonomous apparatuses are central to an understanding of the developing ego of the adolescent, to these two should be added a third: the autonomy of the ego to be responsive to the desires, abilities, unique talents, identifications, dreams, values, and ideals located within the self, that is, within that core of narcissistically cathected self-representations that contain the individual's genetic history of the unfolding of object relations through each successive stage of development (Coppolillo, 1980).

Considerable disagreement still remains among theoreticians in the location of the ego ideal, whether in the realms of the ego and superego systems or in the structure of the self. However, almost all concur in the view that the character of the ego ideal changes dramatically as development proceeds from infancy through adolescence. In an early paper Lampl-de-Groot (1962) emphasized both the ego ideal's location within the ego and its early origins in the narcissism of the infant. He attributed to it a wish-fulfilling function, stating that the infant's capacity to hallucinate a pleasurable tension-reducing state, in the absence of the need-gratifying object, brought him an enhanced self-regard. After the tumultuous upheaval of the oedipal phase, which ushers in the amnesia and massive repressions that veil the first five years, most authors posit a relatively stable, structure-building phase of development through the latency years. Herein the major task is to desexualize the attachments to the same and opposite sex parents and to begin to invest one's energies in the larger social radius of school, community, and peer culture (Hartmann & Lowenstein, 1962).

Thus, more autonomous elements of an ideal self gradually emerge as the young child becomes more differentiated from the parents via his adaptations. This rudimentary ego ideal consists of the infant as a partial regulator of his own tension states; an oedipal self which values remaining loyal and loving to each parent (attitudes substantially bolstered by reaction formation, repression, intro-jection, and displacement defenses); and an eight-year-old self which is esteemed by others for her hobbies, skills, classroom abilities, and capacities to be either a meaningful contributor to the peer group or a leader within it as the situation requires.

The Ontogeny of the Ego Ideal

Other increments to the ego ideal are rooted in the toddler's and preschool child's experiences in the separation-individuation substages of development (Mahler et al., 1975). The practicing toddler achieves a heightened sense of self-worth in his successful ambulating forays into the environment, in large measure aided by a maturing musculature and premature emotional self-sufficiency. The affective experience of elation in this love affair with the world (Greenacre, 1960) and subsequent hypercathexis of the body self add feeling elements to the ego ideal of which mastery and competence (White, 1959) are the cornerstones. Even when the mood is dysphoric, as is evidenced in the ambitendent behaviors that characterize the rapprochement child (Mahler et al., 1975), parent-toddler inter-actions can be self-enhancing. Thus, a toddler by effectively managing his emo-tional distance when rescued on darting away or when treated tenderly by his too close hovering or shadowing mother, has successfully negotiated his separa-tion anxieties. He has erected a self-image that says in effect, "even though I am temperamental and insecure my parents love me more than they dislike my dis-agreeable whining." Titrating his fears with small doses of attachment-specific behaviors, as he relates to the parents of separation, he literally operationalizes a gradually maturing, emergent capacity for affect regulation.

No discussion of the genealogy of the ego ideal would be complete without a review of Blos's tour de force contributions (1962, 1967, 1970, 1972, 1974). The ego ideal is tied to the successful resolution of the negative oedipal constellation, that is, to a reworking of the object love directed toward the parent of the same sex and the subsequent identification that replaces its active expression (Blos, 1970). The male, in particular, relinquishes his passive homosexual position, identifies with the same sex parent's strength, and in doing so, desexualizes both relationships. The result is a mature superego whose tyranny is lessened by an expanded ego ideal that becomes a force in its own right, within the ego, to provide direction and guidance in two primary areas of behavior. These are in late-stage adolescent heterosexual strivings that exemplify the capacity for tender love (intimacy) and attest to the values, when successfully pursued, that will typify competence in the world of work and vocational choice. This transformation retraces the child's steps through the first oedipal period, age 3–5, and the second individuation experiences, ages 12–15. For both male and female the resulting adolescent ego ideal, the mature heir of the negative oedipal complex, coexists with a body image based not on the sexual immaturity of childhood but on the full sexual fertility and potency of the adult (Kestenberg, 1980). In summing up his formulations, Blos remarks that the ego ideal is more personal than the superego and lacks its uncompromising tyranny.

By the final substages of adolescent development, closely approximating Erikson's moratorium (1968), the ego ideal will have attained its status as an institution, located within the ego, that carries its own history of object and self-representations, based on identificatory and introjective processes, from each preceding stage of development. It will have become a guiding force in the pursuit and attainment of mature goals predicated, libidinally, on the dictum, I-love-what-I-want-to-be. Violations of these standards will evoke a sense of self-defeat, embarrassment, shame, or consternation (Piers & Singer, 1971).

Where serious oedipal trauma has resulted in weakened psychic structure and where transmuting internalizations of archaic parental images and the grandiose self into narcissistic cohesiveness have not prevailed, the ego ideal will remain a grandiose and inoperative structure. Pervasive, cumulative narcissistic trauma would be the background of serious ego ideal pathology. Such pathology—associated with massive repression, overwhelming anxiety that is rooted in a deep sense of guilt, and masochistic inhibition—can be seen clinically in adolescents whose ego ideals have failed to mature. Their regressive behaviors stand in stark contrast to the greater maturity displayed by age peers who continue to perform well in school, maintain appropriate friendships, and remain contributing family members even though they may still show signs of struggle with the same adolescent normative development crises. In fact, where such arrests in ego ideal development have occurred, the ego ideal and the superego may have actually merged. Dominating this clinical picture would be identification with the aggressor, self-destructive acting out (the core of a negative identity), and impaired reality testing with wish-fulfilling impulsivity.

Although couched in drive and ego psychology concepts, and the tripartite model of structural theory (S. Freud, 1914; Gedo & Goldberg, 1973), the first psychoanalyst's rambling essay on narcissism contains many profound statements that remain the cornerstone of clinical understanding of narcissistic conditions. First and foremost, a narcissistic individual is incapable of truly loving another. This is so because the narcissist has "hypercathected" his own ego with libido, choosing to love self in preference to external objects. Second, because interpersonal relationships with others serve the purpose of self-aggrandizement and exploitation, the narcissist cannot be fully heterosexual due to the idealized other being modeled on his own physique and body image. Third, Freud suggests that because the narcissistic individual has fueled his psyche with ego libido as well as with the object libido that he otherwise could have invested in others, his ego functions themselves—impulse expression, reality testing, self-esteem regulation, and so on—have become skewed toward idealization, overestimation, and self-indulgence at the expense of objectivity and accurate perception of self and others. In sum, narcissists lack capacities for concern and empathy for others—their sense of time, pursuit of pleasure, and their own needs in general are more important than anyone else's. Pre-oedipally fixated, Freud described their sexuality as autoerotic—as a perversion, the narcissist's sexuality with partners is closer to masturbation than a mutually shared opportunity for stimulation and enjoyment in the experience of orgasm. For Freud, narcissistic love is selfish love.

Primary narcissism on the other hand, as described in the same Freud (1914) essay, is non-pejorative self-love, self-interest, and self-concern and is entirely normal as a prerequisite for survival and further development over the course of life. In normality, both ego libido and object libido are equally distributed within the psyche. The former provides the personality system and its various functions with the requisite drive energies to function, while the latter permits cathecting objects in the external world for relationship purposes that will promote future maturation of the ego through object finding. The resulting identifications contribute to the integrating of the ego as object and self representations accrue from these internalizations. However, when object libido is withdrawn from these external attachments to others, typically as a result of relationship ruptures or trauma, the same libido is reinvested in the self system, thus transforming what was originally reserved for the pursuit of relationships into pathological secondary narcissism. In this fashion relationships atrophy from lack of use. The above sequence depicts secondary narcissism as an object relations pathology. Its key features are a fear of loss of love and the increased insecurity and shame that result from relationship ruptures in the child's early experiences with caretakers. Freud's model of pathological narcissism *in statu nascendi* points to the vulnerability inherent in investing object libido in relationships where external others fail to reciprocate, especially where there is potential for exposure to psychic assault at the hands of significant others. Freud's model contributes to an understanding of the narcissist's egocentric outcome.

Furthering Freud's treatise on the normal aspects of narcissism, he observed that everyone becomes self-centered in a retreat from relating to others when they become physically ill or engage in reverie. Creative people, and gifted athletes in particular, whose special talents or athleticism make them extraordinary, may be more naturally narcissistic than others—when the heavyweight boxing champion of the world, Muhammad Ali, proclaimed, "I am the greatest!" he was absolutely correct in his self-evaluation.

In describing the state of being in love as object libidinal, in contrast to object relations that are narcissistic or anaclitic (the model of dependent relationships predicated on the "man who protects and the woman who tends"), Freud (1914, p. 67) noted that true love involves a mature overestimation of the qualities of the love object as opposed to narcissistic love which pseudo-idealizes, exploits for simple need gratification, and demands admiration of the self. Similar to sublimation, the investment of object libido in a love relationship, defined as "object libidinality," eventually enriches the personality with an identification wherein another's life has become at times even more important than one's own. Thus, to both fall in love and to remain in love, over time, require that the individual relinquish his narcissism, overcome it, and mature both within it and beyond it (Kernberg, 1980). For example, in the movie *The Untamed Heart*, the actor Christian Slater on the occasion of his own birthday celebration brings a gift to the party for his girlfriend, the actress Marissa Tomei. In contrast, Freud pointed out that in pathology, the narcissistic individual idealizes himself and tends to love, exclusively, who she is, what he once was, whom she aspires to eventually become, or someone whom he has experienced as an extension of himself, as once a part of the self.

Narcissism and Ideals: Self Psychology

The groundbreaking *Analysis of the Self* (Kohut, 1971) was written in the cultural context of the late 1960s, 1970s, and 1980s, during a time of significant changes in the fabric of American society. These societal trends included a populace that had gradually become increasingly preoccupied with personal success and fulfillment through the attainment of status, power, and material comforts. This search for recognition and confirmation from others glorified slim, trim athletic bodies, the appearance of eternal youth, and plenty of "flash and cash." The prevailing attitude of the "me" generation was one of entitlement, that is, the expectation that rewards would come easily and that health, wealth, and prestige were guaranteed without necessarily being earned the "old fashioned way," that is, through hard work, diligence, perseverance, and the discomforts attendant to delayed gratification and frustration. Concomitant with these trends was the ever expanding "sexual revolution" with increased sexual license (e.g., "open marriage"), a loosening of moral codes, and freedom to engage in intercourse solely for the pursuit of pleasure as long as these casual relationships with partners were consensual. Bras were burned, "see through" blouses became the fashion statement of the day, rock stars exhibited their genitals on stage in public (e.g., Jim Morrison of The Doors in March 1968, at the Dinner Key Auditorium, Miami), and full frontal nudity and frank sexual acts were to become commonplace in the movies. In this fashion, narcissism began to lose its significance as solely a pathology and became normalized in the context of the "me" generation's embrace of this new liberality. This population of "baby boomers," young adults in their twenties and thirties, sought to unshackle themselves from the old traditions and constraints of their parents who had raised their families after returning home from the Second World War. As relationship needs and self issues were legitimized within a "me" generation culture, the new theory proposed by self psychology expanded narcissism to include a line of normal development rather than solely as a view of personality pathology that connoted flawed character structure as had earlier been proposed by Freud.

The theory of self psychology explains personality development over the life span as a continuous process of the integration and internalization of selfobject functions that serve to organize, at first concretely and then more symbolically, the multiple poles of the self system. One of the key tenets of self psychology involves the role of the self in interaction with selfobjects, defined as external others who are experienced as part of the self and who provide a variety of need-satisfying functions, for example, comfort, soothing, regulating, and protection. The need for these selfobjects in the life of the individual from infancy and childhood, and even through adulthood, is never completely outgrown even though the functions that they serve gradually mature as they achieve increased structural stability through the process of transmuting internalization. Hence, a second basic tenet is the significance of objects in all aspects of the self system in social relations with the self. In this fashion self psychology is a theory with a solid ecological perspective on growth and development in the context of the environment.

The nascent or fledgling self at the beginning of life arrives with a set program for the future, a template that will guide the development of the self system. The self at birth is invested with primary narcissism and the basic drive core of aggression and libido that prioritizes self-preservation through the meeting of basic needs for physical and emotional growth. This nuclear self, present at birth, also includes the constitutional and inherited innate givens that are unique to everyone and that will ultimately shape the individual's self development over the entire life course. These unique factors of course vary with the individual but may include physiological attributes, talents and skills (e.g., superior hand-eye coordination or athleticism), capacities for endurance even when fatigued, a temperament that is naturally easygoing versus uptight and fussy, or a strong immune system that mobilizes quickly to fight off invading viruses and infections. This aspect of the self system, the innate givens that serve to protect or to place the individual at risk, contains the potentials for his future adaptation or eventual dysfunction.

In further specifying the innate givens, the formative pre-wired patterns that await activation and eventual refinement through human experience, five separate emergent motivational systems, or need states, have been described as part of the nuclear self core: (1) the need for psychic regulation, (2) the need for attachment and later affiliation, (3) the need for exploration and assertion, (4) the need to react adversely through antagonism or withdrawal (or both), and (5) the need for sensual enjoyment and sexual excitement (Lichtenberg, 1989). While framed in the parlance of normal developmental need states, each of the above motivational systems provides an entree into clinical issues with the vast majority of adolescents whom psychotherapists regularly serve.

As a theory that underscores the interpersonal context of development, self psychology also retains an intrapsychic focus on the development, maintenance, and regulation of self cohesion through the elaboration of the tripolar selves in interaction with the unfolding of the nuclear self which eventually consolidates at the end of the adolescent stage of development. The third basic tenet of self psychology refers to the structure of internalized representations that make up the core of the structure of the self. These self representations that accrue over time do not constitute, per se, the totality of the self within the larger context of the personality—they are not simply additive. Rather, the totality of the self in self psychology is significantly greater than the sum of its parts as a package of self representations: the cohesive self is the initiating and motivating force that provides purpose, direction, harmony, and coherence to all aspects of the functioning personality.

In addition to the "pre-wired," innate givens housed in the multiple apparatuses at birth (physiology, constitution, genetic traits and potentials, and a primary narcissism that prioritizes survival), the template for advancement through the successive stages of infancy, toddlerhood, latency, adolescence, and adulthood specifies which particular selfobject experiences will come to define the tripolar self. This tripolar self consists of the idealized parental imago, the grandiose self, and the twinship (or alterego) poles. While all three poles of selfobject relating are contained within the template, their actual future organizations as self structure and as functioning elements within the self system are totally contingent on the unique fit between the individual and the caretaking environment. These outcomes of self-structure in all three poles, and in all regards, are acquired through relationships with selfobjects who participate as soothing, regulating, mirroring, idealizing, and empathizing others in the social environment.

The twin poles of self development initially proposed by Kohut were the idealized parental imago pole and the pole of the grandiose self. The former pole reflects the need of the infant and developing child for parental selfobjects who provide security, protection, and safety. Although an archaic idealized imago early in life, the selfobject's functions of soothing in times of stress and regulating of dysphoric psychic and physical states, mediated by idealized parental caretakers, are gradually and incrementally internalized as self structure by the

Narcissism, Character Formation, and Separation-Individuation 37

developing toddler. The selfobject function of mirroring plays a significant role, too, as the child receives validation and affirmation by the idealized parent. In the realm of the grandiose self, the infant basks in the reflected glory of the parent who attunes to her inherent sense of superiority and omnipotence. This archaic selfobject internalization also gradually attenuates as the developing child tempers his primitive exhibitionism and arrogance. With maturation, he will eventually develop a more realistic appraisal of the self leading to mature self-esteem and confidence. All of the selfobject functions, so pivotal in the developing grandiose self of the child, require parental empathy, optimal frustration, and affirmation based on mirroring. Over time, and through the process of transmuting internalization, structure building accrues, bit by bit, and eventually results in a sense of competence based on the individual's actual achievements (Tolpin, 1971).

Such internalizations, in both the realm of the idealized parental imago and the grandiose self poles of self development, will gradually mature into the ideals and the values that serve to guide the adolescent in his interpersonal pursuits and in expressions of ambition based on adaptive capacities to compete and achieve success. While Kohut clearly emancipated self psychology theory from the shackles of Freudian drive psychology, it is interesting to note that he described the idealized parental imago pole as fueled by libido, as one is led by one's values, while the pole of the grandiose self is fueled by aggression as one is pushed forward by ambition. We love our values but we compete to be successful.

It is in the adolescent stage that the third pole of self development finds expression, especially in peer-related pursuits. The twinship or alterego pole refers to the intrinsic need to feel connected and identified with others who are experienced as being the same as us. This structure within the tripolar self reflects a wish for belonging to a group, or a clique of significant others, friends, and peers who share the same interests, values, attitudes, and goals. This pole is operationalized by membership with an "in group" that is polarized vis-à-vis a binary, all-or-nothing "out group" of ostracized others. In this manner the splitting defense mechanism that separates good and bad object and self representations has been elevated from individual dynamics to the level of group process. The "in group" experience is exclusive with a membership that denigrates others. For example, the "jocks" rule and wear similar clothes bought at the same department store, advertise their prowess with their letter sweaters worn on the same day of the week, share similar values with a common language, and serve on the same high school committees. The "out group"—whether yuppies, preppies, computer nerds, squares, or druggies—serve as their foil. While initially functioning as a primitive statement of the need for kinship in the narrow sense within a clique, the advanced-stage adolescent, on the brink of adulthood, will come to embrace all of humankind with a sense of brotherhood that bonds all humans to one another in a collectivity.

In summary, as a developmental theory, self psychology posits the innate givens of a nuclear core self that undergoes continual revision through all stages in the life cycle. The cohesive self involves a reworking of the tripolar selves— the idealized parental imago, the grandiose self, and the alterego—to create a self organization that maintains itself and is harmonious and vigorous, eventually becoming the initiating center of the entire personality. The transmuting internalizations of the selfobject functions, that is, the initially archaic selfobject nuclei (Gedo & Goldberg, 1973) representing parents, caretaking, and significant others, gradually become increasingly symbolic and autonomous. These three poles reflect the guiding values and influence the object choices to which the late-stage adolescent will commit relative to love and work (the idealizing pole), the ambitions that will drive him to succeed (the grandiose self pole), and the memberships he will choose to affirm his connectedness to others (the twinship pole) in friendships, sports, community groups, and other various and sundry affiliations. Thus, self psychology proposes (1) a line of normal personality development over time; (2) a statement of dynamic processes that produce functional change in self structure that is initially archaic in form to one that is fully mature, that is, a self in formation that is capped by a state of self-cohesion; (3) a self in conflict with the drives, internal values, or sense of reality all of which are diagnosable and which lead to expectable transference manifestations; and (4) a self that has transcended conflict and creatively expresses itself with wisdom, humor, natural talents, empathy for others, and an awareness of one's personal transience.

Empathy, Intersubjectivity, and Neurobiology

The narcissistic or selfobject transferences in self psychology theory consist of the merger, mirror, and idealizing transferences, all three being manifestations of impaired cohesive self function in clients whose early relationship experiences in the holding environment of infancy and childhood have been marred by unattuned caretakers with failures, therefore, to form secure attachments. These attachment conflicts in the realm of the idealized parental imago typically involve unempathic responses to the needs of the child to feel protected, secure, safe, and connected in the presence of all-powerful parents whose admirable qualities she will attempt to emulate as she matures into adulthood. The merger transference, which is a somewhat more archaic form of narcissistic selfobject need, refers to the activation in the treatment relationship of the deficits in the pole of the grandiose self with expectations of unconditional approval by the clinician for one's inherent superiority and support for one's exhibitionistic displays and perfectionism. The mirror transference, on the other hand, reflects the client's wish to be acknowledged and affirmed as valued, competent, and esteemed. Somewhat less frequently encountered in psychotherapy is the twinship selfobject transference, which manifests the client's wish to be experienced as identical to the therapist. While portrayed in the self psychology literature as "pure" subtypes, all of these selfobject transferences have variants that appear in one form or another in virtually every psychotherapy where narcissistic conflicts exist, even though there may be a single prevailing mode of transference relating. In sum, which of the selfobject needs will emerge in the narcissistic transferences is determined by the myriad functions of the self for cohesion, stability, and maintenance involving regulating, soothing, idealizing, admiring, and mirroring essential others. However, none of the manifestations of impairment to self structure that emerge in the transference relationship will be therapeutically resolved without the deployment of clinical empathy as the most consistent, salient, pervasive, and enduring mode of communication in the bipersonal field.

The empathic mode (Fossage, 1998) operates on all levels of awareness—conscious, preconscious, and unconscious—and reflects the accurate perception of the client's display of affect states, for example, the categorical affects of anger, fear, sadness, joy, shame, and embarrassment as well as their more subtle variations (Tomkins, 1962, 1963). These emotions in the client may be consciously in his awareness or not—the empathic mode of listening, however, operates to detect nonconscious feelings that are nonetheless present in the client's here and now "felt experience" (A. N. Schore, 2003) The attuning therapist also detects underlying moods that may also be concealed, ones suggesting a substrate of anxiety, guilt, or depression that colors the client's presentation.

Beyond recognizing emotions in the client based on the experience of knowing one's own feelings, "vicarious introspection"—the mode of empathic attunement to the intrapsychic world of the client—begins with the therapist's identification with the client and a capacity for mindsight (D. J. Siegel, 1999). Defined as self-knowledge, mindsight develops in the context of an early, secure base of attachment to caregivers and presumes that the child's working model of the mind of the mother was preceded in time by the parent's working model of the mind of the infant. In reciprocal fashion, autonoetic learning—developing mindsight into the workings of one's own mind—is a necessary but not sufficient condition for knowing the minds of others, including one's own clients. From a slightly different perspective, a capacity for "reflective functioning" promotes a greater grasp of the nature, depth, and quality of one's own affects (Fonagy et al., 2002). As the reflective function further evolves, so too will enhanced affect regulation, including an awareness of the subtle variations that occur in the range of one's own feelings as well as an appreciation of the emotional effects of one's feelings on others. Thus, the empathic mode in the treatment relationship provides a subjective focus on the experiences of the patient as the therapist vicariously introspects in order to comprehend their meanings. All three perspectives are used to arrive at an understanding of the clinical material: the subjectivity of the therapist, the subjectivity of the client, and the inherent intersubjectivity of each as contributors to the co-created transitional space, in between and in the "analytic third" (Winnicott, 1951; Ogden, 1994).

The developmental base for empathy and attuning to the emotions in others on all levels of awareness and in all forms and features of expression—whether verbally, by facial or bodily display, by tone of voice and inflection, or by visual shifts of focus—is laid down early in life. Implicit relational knowing (Lyons-Ruth, 1999) underpins all empathic attunement to others—the experiences of "feeling felt" (D. J. Siegel, 1999) in a secure attachment relationship with caregivers enables the developing child and therapist-to-be to affect-regulate, introspect, and perform mental time travel both to the past as well as into the future and eventually come, thereby, to more fully know the minds of self and others. This kind of knowledge, the clinician's mindsight into self and others, models in the transference relationship the connectedness with his first selfobjects, that is, the caretakers who accurately perceived the inner needs of their child for regulating, soothing, and attuning.

The clinician's empathic response to the client is thus a repetition of these processes of engagement and attunement and qualifies as a bona fide, therapeutic contract to share, at an unconscious level, a wide array of emotions that will include painful affects, disavowed states, and the somatic-visceral disregulations of the primary emotions that are represented in the neural circuitry of the cerebral right hemisphere. The empathic therapist, ever receptive to the moment-by-moment sensations and stimulations occurring in the client, attunes to these right hemispheric circuits that reflect the vertical, top-down processing of strong nonconscious emotion, that is, the neural wirings of the brain structures within the orbito frontal cortex, the amygdala, the hippocampus, the limbic system in general, and within the brain stem and the paleocortex with their sensitivity to the viscera. These latter two structures are located at the "bottom" of the right hemisphere and house the neural wirings that transmit sensation, perceptually, from the vagus nerve via the heart, lungs, bowels, and liver (A. N. Schore, 2003). The precursors to all of these cerebral right hemisphere processes in adults are to be found in the everyday, basic emotional experiences in the holding environment that are encoded within the infant's mind during the first two years at the level of prototaxic (H. S. Sullivan, 1953) or disintegration anxiety (S. Freud, 1926). These conflictual states are transmitted from the client to the empathic therapist who nonconsciously attunes to this "interoceptive information . . . triggered by . . . subliminal interpersonal signals" (A. N. Schore, 2003, p. 82).

The conflictual affects displayed by many adolescents with narcissistic traits range from overt shyness, acute sensitivity to criticism, shame, and inferiority on the one hand, to feelings of envy, arrogance, and superiority on the other. Whether "thin skinned or thick skinned" (Gabbard, 2005, p. 488), the former being characterized as introverted, self-effacing, and vulnerable and the latter as outwardly extroverted, charismatic, self-assured, and conceited, pathological narcissism's common ground pertains to the variety of structural impairments to the grandiose self, the idealized parental imago, and to the developing alterego. The therapist's intersubjective orientation permits a process of engagement, capped by the development of a therapeutic alliance which will eventually witness the emergence of one or more of these selfobject needs in a transference relationship.

As the clinician self-regulates and attends to his own conflictual counter-transference discomfort to remain affectively attuned to the preverbal, stressful primary emotions stored in the implicit memory bank of the client, now being reenacted in the treatment dyad through implicit relational knowing (Lyons-Ruth, 1999), he remains in a therapeutically informed and controlled, shared regressed state of uncertainty, ambivalence, and instability (D. B. Stern, 1983). The clinician's tolerance of such difficult dynamic interchanges with his client activates in the treatment hour the lateralized right hemispheric connections that organized the early holding environments for each. The therapist's capacity to both prolong his focus and to endure without disruption at this level of nonconscious, preverbal relating permits the patient to re-experience, as a repetition compulsion, the ruptures of early attachment processes from the past in the context of the present (A. N. Schore, 2003). In this way, the client's current "felt sense" is validated and given meaning with the simultaneous reorganization in the neural circuitry of the various structures of the cerebral right hemisphere, the seat of strong affect. In this fashion, the implicit memory encodings from the first separation-individuation with the caretakers of attachment are effectively modified as less conflictual in the adolescent's second separation-individuation.

The stance of active receptivity, one that models therapeutic empathy, is the hallmark of the clinician's contribution to all of the selfobject transferences. Because the adolescent stage revisits early separation-individuation processes a second time, it of necessity recapitulates its central themes—misalliances, ruptures of attunement, and hemispheric mismatchings from the left to the right where the infant's unregulated affects and subsequent need for connections at the level of "feeling felt" were processed with a caregiver's lack of empathy, unavailability, or indifference. Because no infancy or childhood is bereft of conflict or some degree of psychic trauma (Blos, 1962, 1970), virtually all adolescents with clinical presentations who engage in a therapeutic relationship will demonstrate identifiable repetition equivalents that mobilize these attachment patterns as they recreate their early histories, symbolically, in a new relationship where mastery is a potential outcome.

Significant projective identification processes operate within the therapy dyad and sustain the unique unconscious dynamics that pertain to the psychologies of both the clinician and the client. The active receptivity of the therapist to the adolescent's behaviors, gestures, physiological state, facial display and affect presentations, and so on permits the unconscious engagement of the right hemispheric structures of each as the implicit memory traces of uncomfortable, dysphoric states trigger responses at the same shared level of mentation (A. N. Schore, 2003). Such reenactments, mobilized in the selfobject transference/ countertransference configuration, contribute to the core of the working through of ruptures and misattunements from the first individuation phase. These key, dual right hemispheric structures in the dyad are therapeutically activated as "heightened therapeutic moments" (A. N. Schore, 2003, p. 82) and permit a transferential selfobject figure to contribute to a reworking and repair of the original misalliance ruptures.

For many adolescents whose character traits cluster around a narcissistic core of impairments to self-cohesion and self-constancy, their attitudes and interpersonal styles—whether grandiose, exhibitionistic, and conceited on the one hand or hypersensitive to criticism, introverted, and self-effacing on the other—serve the purpose of defense against a host of internal-world painful, discordant affect states. These repressed emotions represent the aftermath of insecure attachments and include rage, sadness, envy, shame, and embarrassment—internalizations of the early childhood experiences that are continually reenacted in current object relating. Failures of empathy in these current relationships, the chronic inability of the narcissistically afflicted adolescent client to resonate with the feelings of others, is perhaps their most notable feature. This emotional unavailability and lack of connection to the feelings of others perpetuates, from passive to active expression, similar relationship experiences from their infancies and childhoods, reinforcing non-reflective working models of the minds of self and others (Allen et al., 2008).

The orbito frontal cerebral cortex in the right hemisphere functions to integrate the experience of emotion at the basic level of arousal, stimulus appraisal and perception, somatic representations of bodily experience in the autonomic nervous system and the brain stem circuits, and the encoding of meaning within the neural circuitry. When a pervasive pattern of misalignment of these right hemisphere processes has occurred between the infant/child and the caretaking parents, relational knowledge will be profoundly impaired and the capacity to mentalize self and others becomes severely restricted. As a dismissing parent elicits a shame response in the child, these states of despair tend to be reactivated and engrained, "what fires together, wires together" (Hebb, 1949, 70), setting up a habitual pattern of expectations of others to be similar. In this fashion, blocked mindsight interferes with the development of internal working models that function to add stability and reliability to object relations; self-reflection and the capacity to regulate affects also suffer. Narcissistic youngsters with such impairments will be unable to recognize complex feelings in themselves and will be unable to identify similar emotions in others. These failures of empathy by dismissing selfobjects establish a nonconscious perception of others that is both recursive and inflexible, that is, not prone to maximal, adaptive complexity and change (D. J. Siegel, 1999).

Case Illustration

Tall, slim, and dark-haired, somewhat awkward in his gait and slouching when he sat, fourteen-year-old, pubertal Jim was accompanied by his mother on his first visit to the therapist. In private and over the phone, Jim's mother enumerated the primary reasons for the referral: incessant, disruptive fighting with his twelve-year-old sister, general disagreeableness and increased lethargy about performing minimal family chores, uncontrollable nail biting, and an absence of friendships or after-school activities that might otherwise occupy his time more fruitfully than watching television, surfing the net, or playing with his Game Boy. But far and away, the most distressing of all was Jim's failure to keep his word, promises made in seeming good faith but infrequently carried out, usually to his mother, for instance to do his homework, watch over his three-year-old brother, or buy a gallon of milk on the way home from school.

Enuretic throughout his childhood, Jim had been retained in the first grade due to his overall immaturity and lack of mastery of the educational basics in math and reading. Described as quiet and unassertive, he was the frequent scapegoat of his peer group and, until his recent biological changes and spurt of growth, was often bullied on the way home from school. A marginal student in the early grades, Jim's new environment of the eighth grade (the family had recently moved to the Midwest from a large southeastern city) was already looming large as a formidable barrier prior to his entering high school. Sensing her son's insecurity, exasperated with his uncooperative stance at home, and fearful of his potential for self-defeat, Jim's mother and father both realistically sought treatment for their son. They maintained a cooperative, respectful distance from the outset of therapy, permitting in turn the formation of a therapeutic alliance that was to span the entire academic year and two summer vacations.

The clinical assessment, in addition to the history provided by his mother, suggested a withdrawn, rather passive-aggressive and self-effacing youth whose infancy and childhood development lacked the predisposing correlates of severe pathology reported elsewhere: borderline neurocognitive deficits (Palombo & Feigon, 1984), major affective disorder and bipolar depression (Toolan, 1962; Barton & Martin-Days, 1982), or delinquent character formation (Johnson, 1949; Kaufmann & Heims, 1959; Grossbard, 1962).

Quiet, squirming, and anxious initially, Jim responded to the therapist's first questions and quickly became more relaxed as the structure of the interview minimized painful silences and reassured the youth of this adult's good will. At the close of this first contact, Jim's mother handed her son his coat and motioned for him to leave, but prior to exiting the waiting room she called out to the therapist that Jim had something urgent to tell him: he wanted to make sure he would have appointments, five months away during the Christmas holidays, even though he would be visiting his favorite grandfather for at least a week. Reasoning that this was active expression of a passively feared separation equivalent, as well as a test of his credibility, the therapist responded with the reassurance that he would be Jim's therapist now, and during the holidays and, for that matter, whenever he was needed as a counselor or just as someone with whom to talk.

The initial phase of Jim's treatment during the first six months followed the model of a regressive recapitulation of the separation-individuation phases of the early dyadic period of development (Blos, 1970). The clinical material dealt with Jim's relationship with his mother who continually emerged as a controlling, punitive, irrationally irritable, and uncompromising disciplinarian. Her son, on the other hand, portrayed himself as the victim whose punishment was entirely out of proportion to the infractions. If only the therapist would side with him, they could both get her to leave him alone. Jim's transference to his therapist during this phase was based more on an identification with an older brother/favorite uncle rather than with a distant authority. By providing support and encouraging open discussion, Jim was able to work through his autonomy-threatening dependence on his mother. Even when he was obviously absorbed in his own fantasies and was uncommunicative (rare occurrences), he maintained a uniformly positive transference orientation throughout this phase of his fifteen-month treatment.

This initial phase eventually witnessed a much improved relationship with his mother and a variety of displaced maternal figures—female schoolteachers and Jim's much maligned younger sister who was the embodiment, in his envious eyes, of feminine meticulousness, etiquette, scholarship in the classroom, promise keeping, and the Girl Scout extraordinaire. Second, this phase of therapy also helped to solidify Jim's rudimentary ego ideal of latency. Growth of this self-representational structure resulted in (1) improvement in his school work and skills enhancement (Erikson, 1963), with report cards in the very satisfactory range; (2) increased mastery of some basic social skills, for example, better communication with peers and cooperation on the playground during school hours; (3) the development of an interest in board and computer games, Dungeons and Dragons in particular; and (4) more autonomous after-school play with appropriate-age male peers. These concrete embodiments of ego ideal structure were marred by the breaking of his promises, however, which continued unabated and served to erode the parents' trust in their son. Finally, encouraged by Jim's ability to relate more as a younger friend to an older chum, the therapist as an idealized older brother or favorite uncle helped Jim to shore up his fragile self-esteem. The safety represented by this introject became the basis for the self-transcending of his ego ideal through a magical merger with the therapist, the working through in the middle stage of treatment of the grandiose self and idealized parental imago.

Entry into the middle stage was heralded by an increased, unreachable grandiosity that signaled a major turning point in treatment and a deepening of the therapeutic alliance. The focus gradually shifted from interactions with mother, other females, and school to Jim's relationship with his father. Far from being accessible, however, to exploration and elaboration, as had been his relationship with his mother, this material was only sporadically discussed and seldom in realistic terms.

Arriving uncharacteristically late for his session one afternoon and slouching into his chair in the office with little more than a nod of acknowledgment, Jim's face brightened markedly as his therapist inquired how the weekend had gone. His face beaming, Jim described how he and his father had spent an entire Sunday afternoon together throwing the football, going to a shopping mall, and finally watching an NFL game together on their wide-screen TV. His inflated self-image, as he basked in the warm glow of ideal father-son camaraderie, stood in stark contrast to the reality of that weekend. Earlier that morning Jim's mother, at her husband's urging, had phoned the therapist to describe their continuing disappointment in Jim, who had sulked off to his room after only a few minutes of passing the football and had later refused to watch the NFL game with his father after the opening kickoff. Each had promised the other to set aside that afternoon for each other. Yet Jim's denial of his father's criticism was complete. Instead of chagrin and disquietude, he seemed to wish to believe that his father had only praise for him.

It has been remarked that for the early adolescent girl, a controlled therapeutic regression, and ultimately a full working through of the dyadic separation-individuation conflicts of the first three years, is predicated on the therapist being female rather than male (Blos, 1970; Murphy & Hirschberg, 1982). This prescription rests on the frequently observed transference reactions of the young adolescent female to the male therapist which typically involve the acting out of premature oedipal-phase phenomena and clinical material that focuses on her relationship with the father. What is crucial, therefore, is also missed in treatment provided by a male clinician: drawing into treatment the ambivalence of the daughter toward her mother who must be experienced, regressively and developmentally, once again through the eyes of the two-year-old toddler anxiously separating and regrouping prior to her achievement of adolescent ego autonomy.

No such corollary, however, in the treatment of the young adolescent boy has been espoused (Harley, 1970; Lucente & Mishne, 2010). Clinicians, irrespective of gender, seem uniformly effective in helping most young adolescent males traverse, in symbolic form, these universal strife-laden dyadic conflicts of the separation-individuation substages. However, where disturbance in the father-son relationship existed in the latency years, and where the negative oedipal constellation seems entrenched, it is proposed here that a male therapist will better enable a transference working through of this conflict. Such a working through will have far-reaching implications for the adequate developmental base for attainment of a viable male ego ideal with which to meet the goals of the crucial middle stage of adolescence. These goals would include a beginning psychological emancipation from infantile ties to the family of origin, the intactness of a sexual body ego based on adult genital morphology, and a capacity for meaningful interactions with one's peers—first in all-boy groups, next in mixed male-female situations, and eventually in object choices that approximate the uniform dating experiences prescribed in American culture.

Ten months later, Jim was to show signs of positive movement in all these directions that attest to the acquisition of a more mature ego ideal set of strivings. And most importantly, the elements of the ego ideal that cement mutuality, interdependence, and trust—the social constructions so necessary for a viable interpersonal contract, that is, the keeping of promises—were to emerge and bring to Jim a sense of self-reward as could no other accomplishment. Jim began carrying to sessions his Dungeons and Dragons game, depositing it with his jacket in the waiting room.

Dungeon and Dragons is a game of fantasy and relies upon the player's imagination as no board is used. Two opposing value systems, law and chaos, are in constant struggle with one another. Players choose a character (seven classes) through whom to experience adventures involving ghouls, monsters, evil sorcerers, and dungeons; the prizes afforded winners are experience points and such material rewards as gold and silver coins, magic potions, and equipment. Players win when they successfully defeat the forces of chaos; they lose when they run out of hit points in combat. Each character has preset ability levels with which he starts each game—new characters can be created before starting the next game. Pencils, a character record sheet, six different dice, and lengthy instruction manuals complete the game package. A computer version can also be accessed online.

Finally, weeks later, Jim offered to instruct the therapist on the rules of the game, and, finding a willing partner, for the next few months nearly every treatment session included a round of Dungeons and Dragons. As the intensity and excitement of the games increased, so did Jim's concern for the fate of the therapist in the face of evil sorcerers, dangerous Paleolithic monsters, and dingy subterranean torture chambers. Yet, with a quick toss of the die, or a suggestion, or a blatant change of the rules, never once did the therapist succumb to a fate worse than a missed chance at a reward or a minor detour on the road to success. Jim's grandiosity was in full regalia during such moments and represented a selfobject transference (Kohut, 1971) of his untempered, exhibitionistic needs and unrequited, passive longings for admiration from his father.

Developmentally, these (negative) oedipal feelings were highly overdetermined by the father's long-standing critical distance from his son. Expecting Jim to follow his lead as an avid outdoorsman, athlete, and full-blooded proponent of the dictum *cherchez la femme,* the father, in monthly contacts with Jim's therapist, recounted his disappointment that his son neither pursued girls nor showed an interest in football or baseball. A letterman in numerous high school and college athletics, the father had begun to date at thirteen and desired his son to emulate him in both spheres. These untempered narcissistic demands served to render Jim's oedipal identification with him unstable and tinged with aggression and self-rebuke. This in turn impeded his resolution of the (negative) oedipal constellation and forestalled elevation of the ego ideal to its rightful position as an autonomous structure in his self system.

This material was the core of Jim's active, grandiose position in therapy as the omnipotent hero and director of the fate of the therapist in playing Dungeons and Dragons. As a transference manifestation, it represented the equivalent of a self-transcending through a magical communion with a revered protector. In Loewald's (1980b) terms, the narcissism of the child's ideal ego was being transformed into the more mature ego ideal of mid-adolescent Jim. The less the gratification and self-esteem in interaction with dad at home, the greater was the grandiosity displayed toward the therapist in the transference.

At this juncture, therapeutic interventions relied upon the use of the metaphors inherent in the game (Ekstein, 1966; Allen et al., 2008): protagonists allied with the forces of good in defeating evil enemies and all of the pitfalls encountered by noble warriors in pursuit of glory. Interpretive activity was the order of the day (Harley, 1970; Josselyn, 1971; Meeks & Bernet, 2001; Murphy & Hirschberg, 1982; Lucente & Mishne, 2010). Gradually, Jim began to bring his feelings about his father to the treatment relationship and a working through of both positive and realistically negative elements was effected, in no minor fashion facilitated by monthly educational contacts with both parents as a couple.

A brief explanation is in order for the rationale for treating Jim individually and intensively and seeing, concurrently, his parents in a consultative-psycho-educational context. Each parent had experienced enough trauma in the adolescent years to ill prepare them in guiding their children through the transition to adulthood. However, their considerable ego strength, lack of significant distressing symptomatology, motivation to help their son, and commitment to learning about this stage as a primary preventative to difficulty with their younger children, as well, seemed to assure the feasibility of the plan. It also promoted a supportive stance relative to Jim's investment in his treatment. Reciprocally, Jim found this commitment from his parents reassuring, rather than competitive, and a sign that they were working together on common familial goals. Had therapy for either spouse, or both, been indicated, a referral to another professional would have followed.

The final chapter of Jim's treatment commenced with what Balint has described as a special form of creative communication (similar to his patient's somersault): neither acting out, nor pathological regression, nor symptom of an iatrogenic countertransference-based and unempathic technical error, but instead, a valid nonverbal, client-initiated interaction that repairs, dyadically, in the realm of the "basic fault" (Balint, 1968). In the middle of a session one afternoon, after some rather low-key communication about his beginning interest in field hockey, a class for which he had recently signed up at the local park district, Jim deftly reached into his pocket and pulled out a pair of handcuffs. Walking unhurriedly but with obvious purpose to the therapist, he asked him to hold out his hands, which, after so doing, he locked in place with an unequivocal metallic click. For ten minutes or so the therapy office had a tranquil atmosphere not unlike sitting quietly in a church vestibule waiting for the processional. As therapist and client discussed what had just happened, Jim was of the opinion that he wanted his therapist to know that he would have to trust him completely—amidst some playful bantering and teasing about how difficult it would be to perform some very basic, everyday human operations with cuffed hands—just as he had for over a year now trusted his therapist.

With this explanation, both therapist's and client's hands were uncuffed, literally and figuratively. Jim's magical union with an idealized authority had run its course. The outcome was the attainment of an internalized value system, the more mature mid-adolescent ego ideal set of strivings referred to earlier. The next few months saw Jim gain momentum in typical mid-adolescent activities: mixed male–female group involvements and a chaperoned trip to Washington, D.C., with other teens; sustainment of an avid interest in his sport of choice; and increased mastery displayed in the software games he and his father played on the computer together at home on the weekends.

The Mirroring and Merger Selfobject Transferences

The myriad processes associated with the reflective function, mindsight into self and others, and affect regulation informed all aspects of Jim's treatment as he developed insight into his changing relationships with both parents. I would speculate that, neurobiologically, the right hemispheric structures of the orbito frontal cortex, the limbic system, and the amygdala—and their neural wirings— were all significantly altered through therapeutic activity that increasingly targeted Jim's conflictual affects and fantasies about each parent. In so doing he not only re-scripted his own past childhood narrative, he also began to formulate a new story line, a revised narrative, to continue his autobiography, through adolescence and beyond identity integration into adulthood.

Jim's attachment to me as a selfobject in the initial phase of his treatment centered on his assertion of autonomy as he commenced his emancipation from his tie to the mother of separation. As an idealized selfobject I reflected on his numerous complaints and expressions of frustration in his maternal relationship, empathically exploring with him a wide array of negative affects, the conscious ones as well as their more covert variations contained in his facial grimaces and pouting, the irritation in his tone of voice, and in negativistic body postures. In these attunements, as a selfobject I performed a soothing function as he ventilated and gave voice to his inner experience of her as an irritating, unreasonable, and punitive bad object. The narratives that framed these negative affects usually involved his procrastination with her reasonable requests to attend to household chores and the like. The security and protection I afforded Jim by his internalization of me as an idealized selfobject took place during his developmentally timed second individuation process in early adolescence.

Introspecting on his emotional turmoil with the mother of separation, and attending to his angry affects in interactions with her, enabled him to gain a new perspective on their relationship, that is, that her controlling behavior reflected her own ambivalence with his developing autonomy and her own motivation to infantilize him. As I shared my mentalized version of his mother's fears of losing him to this stage of development and her wish to keep him regressed and infantile, coupled with his newfound sense of being validated and esteemed in the mirror transference with me, Jim's maternal relationship improved considerably as he became more self-observing of his combative attitude and the emotional effects on her of his noncompliant behavior. This improved self-reflective functioning commenced with a fuller awareness of his own affects as well as those he perceived in his mother, especially in regard to her own attachment insecurities. Self-reflecting and becoming more empathic to her at the same time literally changed their relationship as mother and a separating son, one no longer fearful of being engulfed by her as an omnipotent authority.

Explicit mentalizing interventions (Allen et al., 2008) with Jim in the more regressed, selfobject merger transference took the form of narrative storytelling as therapist and client played out their imaginative, pretend roles as warriors and heroes in the game of Dungeons and Dragons. As I resonated with Jim's prevailing affects of intense excitement, hypervigilance in dangerous combat with evil forces, and his sense of power as a victor, I also noticed a concomitant increase in my own heart rate and respiration. I found my own activity level increasing with racing thoughts as I forced myself to concentrate on the images being generated in the game. Jim's cognitive state, almost a flight of ideas with hypomanic elation as he lost himself in the various scenarios, required a match with my own racing thoughts as I attempted to keep pace with his verbalizations, and I found myself becoming increasingly agitated as I tried to keep up with the turn-taking in the rules of the game. At the visceral level of Jim's excitement, grandiosity, and intensity I resonated with the latent, and highly compensatory, features underpinning this manifest display, that is, the shame and humiliation he had internalized and disavowed in an alien self (Fonagy et al., 2002) predicated on his father's long-standing disappointment in his son.

Entering Jim's world of dungeons and dragons and simultaneously "quarantining" my own expectations of what this experience would entail for me (Allen et al., 2008), we abruptly reversed roles as I became the neophyte watching on the sidelines as my young client performed a "clinic" in the nuances of the game, a full command performance on the intricacies involved in a warrior's quest for success and glory. This right hemispheric matching of our affect states, a shared two-person unconscious system (Lyons-Ruth, 1999), permitted prolonged mentalizing interventions that evoked in me an awareness of the implicitly encoded, discordant memory traces of frustration, despair, and futility in Jim's internalized paternal relationship as well as with the peers who had subjected him to the explicitly encoded affects of humiliation and shame with their bullying through so much of his latency years.

Reflecting further on the mentalizing features of Jim's final stage of treatment, it became increasingly apparent to me how overdetermined was his need for being the expert in the Dungeons and Dragons scenarios as a compensation for his sense of inferiority, and how apt had been his unconscious choice of repair, to sense intuitively that his therapist would engage in this indulgence with him as an ally in the countertransference and as a selfobject who would gratify his omnipotent wish for merger. In considering the neurobiology implications, it would appear that the right hemispheric structures—the neural networks of the affect centers in the orbito frontal cortex, limbic system, hippocampal regions, and the amygdala—had meshed with the symbolic themes and imagery in the playing of the game. Communication at this level of emotional experience was analogic and relied on metaphor, creativity, imagination, and vivid, internal visualization. This information-processing mode, unique to the right hemisphere, thus provided "a goodness of fit" with Jim's selfobject deficits, becoming the vehicle for their subsequent repair in the therapeutic relationship.

Jim's maturing three-tiered, hierarchical value system (A. N. Schore, 2003), located in the neural circuitry of the limbic system and serving as an inner guide to his interpersonal relationships, became increasingly evident in this final stage of treatment. Primitive idealizations of self and others, and the grandiosity associated with his internalization of alliance ruptures, were manifest in the transference as repetitions of his interpersonal history with each parent. At the most elemental level of organization were the unregulated affects attendant to tension-laden, hyper-stimulations of the sexual and aggressive drives. These emotional states reflected the unconscious operations of the amygdala and the implicit neural encodings of pleasure and pain that were inferable from his self-indulgence, exhibitionism, and acute anxiety in the Dungeons and Dragons game situation. First and foremost a body ego (S. Freud, 1923), such displays were the observable manifestations of implicit encodings of somato-sensory excitements in the first level, at the base, of the three-tiered limbic system. Neurobiologically, affective experience is global at this first level. At the intermediate level affect expression, which is mediated within the anterior cingulate cortex, becomes more complex and differentiated. Jim's verbalizations of discomfort, resentment, and irritation pointed to a progression in his self-coherence where he could begin to reflect on his own emotions as subjective states of self in interaction with each parent. That he was eventually better able to understand the motivations of his mother's own separation conflicts and his father's egocentric expectations of his son to emulate him suggested a potential empathic base that would engage the top level of the three-tiered limbic system. In this neurobiological model of affect regulation, all three levels of organization flexibly interact with one another to vertically integrate from the bottom to the cerebral top, that is, from the somatic-visceral sensations, to the pre-verbal but higher-order categorical affects, and to the complex meanings that result from neural activity within the preorbital-medial, anterior cingulate, and insula cortex. This three-tiered limbic system, with each tier uniquely dominated by the active presence of mirror neurons, represents the ego and self psychology versions of the ego ideal, the personality structure in each system of thought that shapes the individual's principled engagement of others based on his values, ideals, ethics, and morals.

This three-tiered limbic system model synthesizes neurobiology with psychodynamic personality theory. It incorporates previous stages of moral development, from preconventional to conventional to postconventional (Kohlberg,

1976), and the unconscious and conscious monitoring of behavior through super-ego guilt, with the attendant regulations that are both developmentally ex-pectable at one stage but developmentally impossible at others. Ontogenetically, one's morality is contained in this three-tiered hierarchical system that posits the role of affect—its phenomenology, expression, and regulation—as the dominant mediator between interpersonal experience and intrapsychic organization (A. N. Schore, 2003). Relative to Jim's progress in treatment, his effortful control to "keep his word," implicit in the promises made to self and other, revealed the functioning of his developing adolescent ego ideal.

In the very first treatment hour Jim's fears of separation and loss—potential rejection by a transferential authority—had emerged, in retrospect, as an invita-tion to engage in a therapeutic process. Toward the end of treatment, with his handcuffing me, he symbolically reenacted a whole host of issues that finally brought closure to his search for self-coherence. Verbally attending to his mo-tives for handcuffing me, and with appropriate emotional composure, he calmly, thoughtfully, and eloquently self-reflected on the multiple meanings of his be-havior. In so doing, he displayed a much improved ability to mentalize our rela-tionship and the minds of self and others. His acting out in the therapeutic cul-ture, actually an "acting in," signified a purposeful use of the dyad, a maturing capacity for an agency that spontaneously and playfully demonstrated active ownership of his progress in treatment.

One final observation is in order. His much-desired trip to the capital city was the upshot of Jim's making, and then keeping his promises first to himself, and then to his parents, in three areas: continued concentration in school, affection-ate responsibility in the care of his younger brother during his parent's occa-sional, planned absences, and interest in and pursuit of a sport of his choice. Ter-mination followed shortly thereafter.

Splitting, Differentiation, and Identity

Were I the Moor, I would not be Iago.
In following him, I follow myself.
Heaven is my judge, not I for love and duty,
But seemingly so for my peculiar end.
For when my outward action doth demonstrate
The native act and figure of my heart
In compliment extern, 'tis not long after
But I will wear my heart upon my sleeve
For daws to peck at: I am not what I am.
(*Othello,* Act 1, scene 1, lines 57–65)

The Moor is of a free and open nature
That thinks men honest that but seem to be so,
And will as tenderly be led by the nose
As asses are.
(Act 1, scene 3, lines 405–408)

The Moor, howbeit that I endure him not,
Is of a constant, loving, noble nature. . .
Make the Moor thank me, love me, and reward me
For making him egregiously an ass
And practicing upon his peace and quiet
Even to madness. 'Tis here, but yet confused.
Knavery's plain face is never seen till used.
(Act 2, scene 1, lines 307–313)

Incisive analyses of the exercise of human influence by one party over another are not confined to the pages of clinical journals. In fact, Shakespeare's

Othello (1997) provides as vivid an account as exists anywhere in literature of the capability of one individual to make others play out, regressively, his and their own deepest pathologies. Iago's psychological motivations are tortured and complex. Slighted by Othello, the Moor of Venice and commander of the garrison at Cyprus, conflicted in his marriage to Emilia whom he threatens to murder at the denouement, and envious of Cassio, the lieutenant who has been appointed second in command, Iago uses his relationships with each of the protagonists to coerce them into becoming his puppets to play out his own perverse conflicts. His hatred of Emilia is ruthlessly exploited through Desdemona, as a defensive displacement, as she becomes the embodiment of seductive, feminine infidelity and deceit, and a bad object in Othello's unsuspecting eyes. Othello in turn accepts the projected, hated object representation of the cuckolded husband, and by play's end performs a double murder, Desdemona's and his own, while plotting a third. Cassio is solicited by Iago into drunkenness and brawling, self-besmirching his own carefully cultivated reputation, and the Venetian gentleman, Rodrigo, is enticed into plotting the young lieutenant's murder. All of the above is accomplished through the power of Iago's projective identification processes to exploit, dethrone, and ruthlessly make others conform to his own conflicted psychological script. In so doing, his fantasies become their reality.

The ultimate power of Shakespeare's tragedy rests on the playwright's implicit awareness that human discourse operates on many different levels of meaning and that some conflicts are universal: the quest for power, security from loss, self-cohesion and the need for psychological repair through relationships. While Othello and Desdemona in some ways remain the tragedy's central characters, the actual focus of attention gradually shifts from their characteristics to the guile, subtle use of innuendo, and Machiavellian contortions that showcase Iago's purposeful relationships with the protagonists. Having lost control of themselves and their center in the play, they become deuteragonists to Iago's driving quest for revenge. The play's center thus becomes a psychological field, the part object-part self world, identificatory systems, and changing dynamics of the antagonist in this drama to his foils. In similar fashion, therapist and borderline client traverse a shared psychological terrain where primitive self and object images seek discharge in a relationship tailor-made for such enactments of conflict.

Recent research findings in infant psychology have made possible a more comprehensive understanding of later stages of growth throughout the life cycle, notably adolescence, validating many propositions derived from clinical ob-servations in work with children and adults. Many of the most cherished concep-tualizations of infant process vis-à-vis caretakers have been retained; for exam-ple, the interior representational world of self and object images (Jacobson, 1964), body ego and drive cathexis (S. Freud, 1923), symbiosis, rapprochement crisis, and the individuation track (Mahler et al., 1975), auxiliary ego (Spitz, 1965), and sense of identity (Greenacre, 1958; Erikson, 1968). The following case discus-sions will address the compatibility of these concepts with findings from neuro-biology research. At issue is their applicability to the nature of the early object relations experiences of infant ego with the mother and the relevance of these concepts to the adolescent phase, as a second individuation process, in consoli-dating identity, character formation, self narrative, and affect regulation as well as in client-clinician experience in the treatment dyad.

The object relations literature, attachment theory, ego psychology, and re-cent contributions from self psychology and the intersubjectivists have all de-tailed with increasing clarity how adolescent and adult clients reenact intrapsy-chic conflicts that devolve around dyadic, separation-individuation themes rather than the triadic conflicts of the oedipal phase. The term *splitting* has a venerable history and first appeared in a number of Freud's monographs on the availability of certain defense mechanisms to deflect anxiety, particularly that arising from the threat of rejection, loss of love, painful separations, and abandonment (1940). Of course, many authors have subsequently expanded and modified this original formulation but in virtually every instance, one notable similarity has emerged with striking clarity, namely, that defensive splitting occurs in most dramatic and observable fashion as young preschool children, 16–36 months old, negotiate the coming and going, returning and leave-taking, of their mothers in the rapprochement substage of separation-individuation prior to obtaining object constancy (Mahler et al., 1975; Kernberg, 1966). This particular aspect of object relations theory is most notably dealt with in Mahler's conceptualization of the rapprochement crisis in the third separation-individuation substage subse-quent to symbiotic "dual unity." Splitting occurs with the traumatic realization of the absence of the mother whose "good" but unintegrated maternal part object representation can no longer be maintained in the toddler's conscious awareness when simultaneously juxtaposed to her unintegrated "bad" part object repre-sentation (Kernberg, 1980). Dropped off at nursery school or day care, a rap-prochement stage two-year-old might quickly react to his mother's absence by

screaming and tears but relate to her with a characteristic and subdued detach-
ment upon her return. During the interim, however, this same youngster might
revel in playing in close proximity with a substitute caretaker.

To put splitting in its proper perspective, it should be considered a normal
and developmentally appropriate way, in the young child's object relations, to
organize primitive part self and part object representations. Splitting of the self
and object world is gradually replaced by more advanced mechanisms—projective
identification, introjections, and selective identifications (Greenacre, 1958,
1960)—just as the ambitendent behaviors of the rapprochement stage toddler
serve as significant precursors to post-ambivalent object relations which in turn
promote the capacity for future, more mature relationships.

The shadowing and darting away behaviors of the rapprochement stage
toddler fully operationalize the concept of splitting as an intrapsychic mechanism. Developmentally unable to maintain an integrated and whole object representation of the mother as both nurturing and available, a good part object,
as well as frustrating and absent, a bad part object, the youngster veers away
as if to escape her influence which might, if prolonged, further contaminate his
already highly tarnished image of her as omnipotently all-giving (Mahler et al.,
1975). The ambitendent biphasic behavior, announced by a sudden rush into her
arms, reflects the child's parallel wish for an instantaneous reunion with the grat-
ifying good part object. It, too, is a brief, sporadic, and unpredictable specimen
because such a rapprochement wish would carry with it the potential danger, if
fulfilled, of re-engulfment, that is, a symbiotic merger replete with loss of ego
boundaries and dissolution or fragmentation of the fledgling sense of self.

Attachment-Differentiation: Identity and Character Formation

Karla, age fourteen, was accompanied to the office by her parents who sought
consultation for their daughter's recent theft of clothes and jewelry from a
neighbor's house. Dark-haired, verbal, bright and attractive, this pudgy high
school freshman had pressured her mother for over a year, unsuccessfully, to
permit her to babysit for the two young sons of their neighbor, a breezy, slim-
figured realtor in her early thirties who dressed fashionably and exuded a confi-
dent air of spontaneous charm and sound, good business sense, qualities that
were notably absent in Karla's overweight mother, who in comparison appeared
careless in her dress and matronly in outlook. For one month the babysitting
assignments had seemed mutually satisfying to all concerned. Then came the

neighbor's phone call; the subsequent accusation of the theft was later verified when Karla's upset parents searched her room. Starkly juxtaposed to Karla's verbal denial of the theft was the physical evidence: designer blue jeans and cosmetic jewelry hidden, in only token fashion, on a top shelf in her bedroom closet. While refusing to admit to knowledge of the stolen items, Karla did consent to return them and to pay for some inexpensive earrings that could not be found.

Karla's theft represented more than an acting out of primitive aggressive impulses against a symbolically, but displaced, maternal object. Nor was her act solely an unconscious expression of the ego's barring of painful memories from reaching conscious mentation. What treatment revealed, in the space of three interview hours in the fifth month of a once-weekly therapy, was Karla's wish to establish herself as separate and differentiated, yet similar and bound, to her mother in the second individuation process of early adolescence (Blos 1967, 1970). The theft was symptomatic of this core conflict in the area of her dyadic object relationship with her mother and could be fully understood only in its psychodynamic, genetic-developmental unfolding, as a defensive constellation.

The task of emancipation from her early object tie to her mother was made initially more difficult for reasons beyond Karla's control. Her parents had adopted two infant sons, two and four years older than Karla, and it was only then, subsequent to the adoptions, that the mother had become pregnant. The elder sons, now 16 and 18, manifested a variety of antisocial profiles as delinquents, truants, and drug dealers. Each had received professional attention from concerned school counselors and behavior disorder learning specialists from the early grades on. For Karla's mother, her daughter represented a last chance to achieve any semblance of parental success and social approval. The pressure on Karla was enormous and taxed the biological daughter's adaptive capacities to the limit.

The mother's symbiotic wish had continued to dominate most of her primary maternal set in interacting with Karla, and throughout Karla's latency it was of no concern to the mother that her daughter would periodically take money from her purse without her permission to buy accessories, candy, or movie theater tickets. This behavior was neither discouraged nor rewarded but, rather, a message was subtly conveyed that as an auxiliary, mother's money supply represented for Karla an open cash account which required no receipt for withdrawal. Like the blissful reward of being nursed on demand for her first twelve months, rocked to sleep, or being transported in the snuggly that permitted the libidinized ventral surfaces of each to be in continuous contact with one another, mother and daughter remained in a state of dual unity, of felt need and maternal supply, attenuating rather than concluding their earliest mode of object relationship. Like a toddler in the practice substage of separation, the mother was available for refueling, in this instance the emotional currency being green. While an affective attunement (D. N. Stern, 1985) likely mediated Karla's experience of her mother in the earliest dual unity, her mother's emblematic, that is, narcissistic, primary maternal preoccupation (Winnicott, 1956) in later developmental stages only served to hamper her daughter's individuation process. Indeed, central to the attunement of the holding environment mother is her awareness that facilitating the developing independence of her infant requires her to be empathically unavailable as a soother while at the same time presenting an inner representation that conveys the infant's competence to be able to master conflicts on his own (Winnicott, 1960b).

As Shopper (1984) has pointed out, the early adolescent years for the female (in contradistinction to the experience of the adolescent male) involve an active search for body ego ownership devoid of the narcissistically controlling influence of the mother. In this regard, too, Karla's mother had sought to involve herself in her daughter's genital body management—there were intrusive instructions on menstruation, prohibition of tampon use, an insistence on consultation with her own gynecologist rather than one of Karla's choosing, and vilification of her sons' sexual code of flagrant promiscuity with the warning that Karla remain a virgin or be damned. This blurring of ego boundaries forced Karla to defend against the too close tie to her mother as she simultaneously sought an autonomous and separate sense of self.

Some events in the preceding six months presaged Karla's onset of differentiation conflict. Employed as a morning bus driver for the same high school Karla attended, the mother now, in addition, occupied her daughter's time after school with excursions to suburban shopping malls. She responded to Karla's embarrassment at being seen in her company by high school age mates with an invitation to include her friends on these outings. This seemed in keeping with her utter disregard for her daughter's stage-specific, developmental thrust toward same-gender peer activity away from the family of origin. However, Karla's discomfort was not total. Indeed, it seemed curious to me that she both resented, yet simultaneously felt comforted by, her mother's presence on these frequent, almost daily, shopping ventures.

The meaning of this ambivalence on Karla's part to the symbiotic-like attachment behaviors of her mother became clearer as her unequivocal therapeutic alliance made accessible to verbal discourse her conflicted wishes in treatment. For Karla had never really believed that she was her parent's natural daughter. In fact, her disbelief in her biological heritage was part and parcel of her active search in someone else's family for her core identity as the child of some other couple. This disbelief also explained her insistence on the painful, ambivalent, and insecure attachment to her mother on the shopping trips.

The neighbor husband and wife, whom she scouted out and then chose, had been the focus of her fantasies ever since she turned twelve. Their children, two young sons, revealed to their mother that Karla had frequently questioned whether they had not themselves been adopted. In Karla's mind she reasoned that she resembled their mother far more than her own. She, like Karla, preferred fashionable clothes, was conversant with the music of current hard rock musicians and their milieu, and enjoyed riding in sporty cars rather than in school buses. If Karla's brothers were disappointments to her parents as adoptees, might she not also be able to prove, by the antisocial act of stealing, that she, too, belonged biologically to a different family? Might not that family be this one? And might she not go her brothers one better by actually knowing who her real mother was? Such reversals and contortions of images of identity and differentiation, and attempts to emancipate from her object ties to her parents, were clarified and explored, at first haltingly, and then with more candor, trust, and acceptance.

To the ego's fundamental twin autonomies, from the demands of an impinging environment from without and from the throes of a tyrannical, impulsive, drive dominance from within (Rapaport, 1951, 1958) and, third, to the ego's ancillary capacity to be autonomous to the standards and values reflective of a mature ego ideal (Coppollilo, 1980; Lucente, 1986), a fourth autonomy emerges from the analysis of the symbolism conveyed by Karla's symptomatic search for a new family and her theft behavior within it. This would be the change of one's geographical residence to be more in keeping with an emergent identity (Blos, 1962) and a migration as an adaptive solution in the conflict-free ego sphere (Hartmann, 1939). Karla's fantasy of belonging biologically to different parents reflected her highly overdetermined internal conflict over how to be both different and similar to her mother and how to be both an individual self yet remain loyal to her primary, interiorized object representation. Karla's search for identity involved differentiating from her mother, a variation on the family romance (S. Freud, 1909b) wherein aggressive and libidinal oedipal strivings are safely validated through non-incestuous, extrafamilial longings, and atonement for the acting out of parental superego lacunae (Johnson, 1949).

This last feature of Karla's search for self identity, superego atonement for unconsciously sanctioned parental wrongdoing, emerged when she stated that her procurement of clothes and jewels from her neighbor was to be a gift for her mother if and when she lost weight and became interested in current fashions. That an adolescent might act out the superego pathology of parents via an identification with their asocial strivings is clinical common knowledge. That Karla was subtly encouraged to do so, to take the property of others, was made explicit when she described her father's practice of bringing home, for sale or for his own use, surplus gallons of paint, solvent, and cleaners from the industrial corporation where he worked as a maintenance engineer. Each parent, the mother by silent approval and the father by direct example, thus unwittingly fostered an unintegrated superego development in their youngster. The reversal from guilty thief to kindly benefactress represented the active side of Karla's fantasy of reparation and rescue. Karla's fantasied mini-migration to another family, rather than a regression, thus reflected elements of autonomous strivings to be free from the tensions of a too close tie to her parental objects.

Identification and Differentiation in Treatment

It was stated emphatically by Jung (1961), whose profound writings covered the self, religion, the soul, archetypes, and the collective unconscious, that the worst that could befall anyone would to be perfectly understood by another human being. While insight-oriented therapy for adults is the model for this age group around which parameters, or deviations from the interpretive mode, are gauged, the above considerations do not, even remotely, apply to adolescents, especially young adolescents. Self-understanding can be better achieved, rather, by a careful process of exploration and an empathic concern for a too early disclosure of emotional turmoil. Affect attunement (D. N. Stern, 1985), mentalizing, and the bridging of subjective experiences (Fonagy et al., 2002; Allen et al., 2008) are concepts that apply to the experience near clinical reality of work with young adolescents. Adolescents simply do not trust adults who desire to know them too soon and with too much curiosity.

This was especially true of Karla, whose first three months of treatment were devoid of any mention of her theft of property from her maternal surrogate of displacement. Such a treatment approach emphasized the present, reality-oriented interests and pursuits of this verbal youngster: her favorite rock musicians, friends, and teachers, clothing preferences, her summer work as a candy stripe hospital volunteer, and her centripetal relationships with parents and brothers. Ego functions—defenses, self-esteem, adaptive strivings, reality testing, affect expression, cognitive mode, and impulse control—were all assessed, quietly. And most of the interpretive work was a one-way communicative street, from clinician to clinician rather than from clinician to client. Paradigmatically, the therapist self engaged the adolescent self in a process of slow revelation through exploration and discovery, each session expanding or retracting, as needed, the space between boundaries of the selves in interaction with one another.

Entering the middle stage of treatment, I began to notice that Karla would refer to her peer relations more frequently in sessions, shyly remaining vague and distant as I inquired about her friendships. From her hesitation to disclose, I intuited an underlying tension that was not unlike her initial ambivalent attitude toward her mother's preoccupation with their shopping excursions to the mall. In middle school her "in group" had consisted of four close friends who now were avoiding her "like the plague." All of her efforts to reconnect with her friends and return to her former inner circle seemed only to bring more ostracism and a mounting sense of urgency in the face of this peer rejection. To make matters worse, her former friends taunted and ridiculed her, hurling invective as well as spreading unflattering rumors about her to anyone who would listen. The verbal attacks were becoming more personal with criticisms about her appearance— wardrobe, hairstyle, and makeup. Karla vacillated between outrage and sadness during these difficult weeks of unrest, and her affects were almost palpable as I empathized with her frustration over the loss of connection.

Gradually, one of her friends reached out, communicating in detail her own escalating conflicts with her parents in their disapproval of her hair color (pink), her jeans (too low-riding and too tight), her eye shadow (too dark), and her recent choice of a boyfriend (seventeen years old, inappropriate, and too risky). Karla's initial reaction, which to her credit she did not indulge except in fantasy in treatment hours, was to seize the opportunity to retaliate in kind, confronting her former friend and vilifying her conduct as a disloyal traitor. Instead, she re-mained receptive and respectful in her role as a sage confidante and safe harbor for her beleaguered peer. Over the subsequent weeks their relationship deep-ened in large measure because of Karla's self-observing of her own range of affects that enabled her to commit to keeping her friend's secrets. In turn, her friend's functioning also improved as she was helped to self-reflect, manage her own feelings, and strategize ways to better communicate with her parents. In short, having mentalized her relationships with her own parents of separation, with increased mindsight into her own motivations and affects, Karla was now able to develop a working model of her friend in interaction with another mother of separation. With varying degrees of success, this process of loyal con-fidante who never once breached the privacy of her communications was re-peated with her other three friends as well, ensuring her readmission into her peer network.

Paradoxically, the source of Karla's emotional vulnerabilities, the prolonged symbiotic attachment to her maternal object and the multiple gratifications that it had afforded her, also provided the base for her highly evolved, adaptive repair of these peer relations. Her early holding environment had been mediated by a mother with an exquisite sensitivity to her infant's needs for soothing, comfort, and emotional regulation. This maternal symbiotic attunement provided Karla with innumerable, implicitly encoded experiences of "feeling felt" (D. J. Siegel, 1999), in a highly empathic form of primary maternal preoccupation (Winnicott, 1956). Mentalizing her infant daughter's various affect states, and accurately re-sponding to them with a congruent match of maternal activities that restored Karla's balance, were all internalized as representational encodings within Karla's cerebral right hemisphere.

Neurobiologically, these "mirror mechanisms" served as a bridge from mother to daughter in the mentalizing regions of the brain—the amygdala, the medial prefrontal cortex, the anterior cingulate cortex, and the limbic system in general where mirror neuron activities are the most prominent. These right hemispheric areas, the resonance circuits described by Trevarthen (1996), are cen-tral for attuning to others with empathy and a capacity for nonconceptual, im-plicit relational knowing, and in fifteen-year-old Karla their neural circuitries were prematurely overdeveloped as potentials for future subject-object match-ing. These internalizations provided the base for evoking in Karla a simulation of the feelings of others (Gallese, Keysers, & Rizzolatti, 2004) leading to her friends' affects being recognized, validated, and understood. Of course, true empathy would require significantly more than the activation of mirror neurons in these right hemisphere sites for the emotional knowing of others. Perspective taking, advanced social referencing, greater self-object differentiation, and a capacity for a more refined quarantining of her own feelings, well into early adulthood, would also be needed in these regards. Yet Karla's adaptive, "effortful control" (D. J. Siegel, 2007, 114; Allen et al., 2008) of her own affect-regulating functions in concert with the mirror neuron activity invoked in these jeopardized peer relationships proved to be indispensable in salvaging them from the point of no return.

While Karla's age-appropriate, in-group experiences with her friends began to replace her enmeshed relationship with her mother, frequent shopping excursions to the mall remained a significant feature of her social life and, in retrospect, continued to affirm her emergent identity. On one of these ventures to her peers' favorite fashion boutique, Karla was detained by mall security officers as she exited the fitting room and passed the checkout station to exit the store. In her shoulder carry bag they found three tops, none of them her own size. Contacted by cell phone, Karla's mother immediately rushed to the store, and, because Karla had remained on the premises, had cooperated fully and because she agreed to purchase the items, no charges of theft were forthcoming, although she was barred from shopping there for the next six months. In therapy hours we explored Karla's fantasies surrounding her acting out. These included her motive wish to be perceived as a generous friend selflessly indulging others at her own expense and self-defeating at one and the same time. At the level of defense, her shoplifting of the tops for her friends was illustrative of the mechanism of identification through altruistic surrender (A. Freud, 1946). The theft also signified her quest for alterego self objects, that is, needs for an identity shared with others as a "we self" in an illusory orbit of connection. Finally, the themes of attachment-differentiation from her maternal imago, on the deepest level, attested once again to a solution through action, a simultaneous acting out and repetition-compulsion replay of her continuing unintegrated identity conflicts to individuate and eventually become whole.

From peer rejection and loss, from defensive avoidance of any contact with her ostracizing friends, and from separation anxiety to individuation retraced the central themes of her rapprochement crisis (Mahler et al., 1975) with her mother. The revisiting of these individuation issues afforded Karla yet another opportunity for a resolution of the original conflicts. Over-identifying with her friends' predicaments with their family members and with their romantic entanglements with boyfriends was a defensive reaction, initially, that served to repress her anger at them, splitting her object and self representations into "all good and all bad" extremes. These two defenses also reinforced her conscious solicitude and concern for them as reaction formations designed to hide her underlying irritation. However, as Karla reflected on these underlying affects, she became increasingly focused on the ambiguous and conflict-laden moment by moment, "blow by blow" features of the narratives presented to her by her peers for guidance and direction. These heightened social experiences, ones mediated by continuous activity in the anterior cingulate cortex with mirror neuron involvement in all of the right hemisphere affect centers, eventually transcended defense and were replaced with the emerging character traits of respect, loyalty, and compassionate concern as they became enduring elements of her interpersonal style in peer friendships. It is noteworthy at the level of neurobiological functions that these experience-dependent, relational involvements with her peer group that we processed in treatment potentiated bilateral integration of the two hemispheres as the ensuing narratives of self and other combined Karla's right hemispheric affects with her left hemispheric linguistic constructions that are mediated in the dorsolateral area of the prefrontal, orbital neocortex (D. J. Siegel, 2007).

Freud's elevation of the ego in the tripartite model of structural theory (1923) to the center of psychoanalytic discourse can be viewed profitably in concert with his treatise on narcissism (1914). The operative terms are ego, self, and object. Intertwining the two writings, to be narcissistic means one is self-centered as a primary orientation to others. Being self-centered in turn requires the hypercathexis of one's own psychic processes to the exclusion of those of others. That is, object libido available for relationships is first retracted from others, a decathexis, and then diverted to one's self, the effect being a geometric multiplication of the inner-directed investment of ego libido. The empathically attuned clinician does the above regularly, in a state of "evenly suspended attention" (S. Freud, 1912b) accounting for his extraordinary knowledge of clients that comes from this hyperawareness of the therapeutic self in interpersonal interaction. Clinicians thus know their clients by exquisite self-observation of how they think, feel, and ultimately understand themselves in this dual unity. Simultaneously quarantining this internal search of the self with a focus on the client, this knowledge is regularly communicated in some fashion to the client, transcending its narcissistic base and rendering subsequent utterances object-directed and empathic.

The ability to maintain an "evenly suspended attention" (S. Freud, 1912b) to Karla's relational experiences with her mother and her peers was central to my functioning as her therapist. This capacity, an openness to attend without preconceived biases to virtually all that there is to observe in the client's presentation, also includes his "receptive awareness" (D. J. Siegel, 2007, p. 124) to be simultaneously open to his own unconscious responses to the clinical material. This twofold thrust of the therapist's intersubjective awareness of the two selves in the relationship dyad is a byproduct of his intense clinical concentration on affect states, physical sensations, body postures, facial displays, and intuitions as they reverberate within his own unconscious system (A. N. Schore, 2003). This state of mindfulness (Epstein, 2007) defines the clinician's stance of an "evenly suspended attention" and once developed, activated, and maintained over time becomes what D. J. Siegel (2007, p. 164) has described as an "intention to attend." From "effortful control" of this evenly suspended attentional stance, a stable and enduring, ever-shifting and mobile awareness of self and client emerges as the characteristic therapeutic state that informs practice. This stable state of attention, to variously concentrate on the inner experience of the self as therapist in interaction with the client as object, can become an enduring character trait of the "effortless mindfulness" that guides one's orientation to the multiple processes operating simultaneously in the dyad. This capacity for clinical concentration, commencing as a stable state of attention, matures over time and with further refinement and experience changes from a stable state to an enduring character trait of mindfulness—intrapsychically as a synthetic function of the ego, interpersonally as a foundation for intersubjective practice, phenomenologically as a forum for the exchange of affects, and neurobiologically as "what fires together, wires together" (Hebb, 1949, p. 70) further enhances the resonance and attachment circuits of the brain.

After a particularly productive session one afternoon, elaborating the connection between Karla's wish to get to know her neighbor better and the desire to be different from her own mother, I went to my desk to do some mundane written work. Reaching for my favorite pen, a gold-plated Schaeffer ball-point, one of a two-pen paired set, I observed with considerable consternation that it was absent from its rubbed-walnut finished holder. With one gone, the set looked awkward, incongruent, and out of sync, corresponding perfectly with my own feelings of perturbed agitation. It was gone because Karla had surreptitiously placed it in her purse while my focus of attention was diverted to noting her time next week in my appointment book.

The meaningful dialogue that had begun to elicit Karla's thoughts on her theft of clothes and jewelry had been predicated on a self-disclosing communication that was revelatory of my own experience as an adolescent asserting myself against a parental expectation that simply could not be fit into the fabric of my own emerging sense of uniqueness. This experience at the time had been conflictual, mobilizing anguish, arguments, and some acting out. Now it was an ego syntonic memory integrated into my sense of a unique, temporal ordering of identity points and divested of its previously symptomatic meaning. This story was shared with Karla to encourage her identification with me as a narcissistic support (Basch, 1980), a selfobject, one which would strengthen the therapeutic alliance and hopefully enable Karla to reflect on her relationships with her mother and neighbor, and on the disillusioning significance of her theft behavior. In D. N. Stern's terminology (1985), the vignette functioned as a bridge from the therapist's subjective experience of self, as adolescent, to Karla's current subjective experiencing of her mother: this was an expression of the therapist as a transference parent dialoguing, being with, the internalized infant self of his patient.

While achieving the one purpose, that is, self-discovery and validation of her motivations, feelings, and attitudes surrounding the theft, this calculated introduction of the therapist-as-adolescent, an object for identification, produced another but unintended iatrogenic effect, namely, the sense of a shared unity wherein Karla's needs were equated with the therapist's supplies. Just as her mother had once served as a supplier of money and just as Karla had most recently fantasied the neighbor's clothes as her own, the merger implied by the therapeutically motivated identification meant that my pen was also her pen.

Indeed, Karla's reflections on her schoolwork revealed a desire to excel in the classroom and eventually pursue a college education. Such reflections were interspersed with requests, most often gratified with therapist compliance, for information about his own educational experiences leading to professional degrees. This idealization of knowledge represented a significant identification by the adolescent with her therapist in the realm of the ego ideal. It was in this context of a dual unity of a shared symbolic currency—neither money, nor clothes, but knowledge—that Karla took the pen for the purpose of writing her semester-end in-class examinations over a one and one-half week period. Her exams behind her, the pen was returned with a casual statement to the effect that she had absent mindedly borrowed it without any particular conscious thought or ulterior intent.

Discussion

It is widely accepted that effective therapeutic communication requires conversing in the preferred medium of the client: with adolescents, the normative terrain of language, expressive metaphor, and meaning is the narcissistic mode. Therapists who recognize this facet of adolescent self and other experiencing will be more likely to be effective with their clients. An empathic attunement of clinician to client (D. N. Stern, 1985; Ogden, 1994; Atwood & Stolorow, 1999), for this reason, serves a mirroring function, providing a mechanism for self-discovery through reflection and focus. Guided by a theory of intersubjectivity, such attunements enable therapists to reach the clinical infants still residing in their older patients. The adolescent client's discovery of identity, and the identifications themselves that contribute to it, are well served in a therapy climate that promotes a safe exploration of these multiple selves and subjective interpersonal experiences. A therapeutic culture that is intersubjective, rather than one solely for the elaboration of intrapsychic processes, fosters such a safe exploration and replaces the anonymous, blank screen approach with one that promotes an experience near forum for self-discovery (Basch, 1980).

Self-reflection was encouraged throughout Karla's treatment and mobilized in her an appropriate sense of narcissistic entitlement to the omnipotent potentiality of an identification with her therapist. Recognizing that a deepening of Karla's identification with me would achieve this goal and simultaneously permit some emotional distance from the embarrassment generated by her acting out, I used my own self-reflective, introspective stance to resonate with hers in a symbolic state of shared harmony or dual unity. This state of shared harmony was operationalized by a self-disclosing revelation of my own difficulty with a parent in my early adolescence.

As to the significance of Karla's use of her therapist's pen to write exams, one point of view would hold that the pen symbolized the unconscious phallic wish of the female for the anatomically absent penis. This orthodox view would hold that, as a transference phenomenon, Karla's taking of the therapist's possession amounted to an impulsive acting out of the negative side of her ambivalence in the treatment relationship and a major resistance to her therapy, presaging an ominous future negative therapeutic reaction to interventive work. A variation on this theory would hold that, even if she had no such desire to possess a penis for herself, no one else should have one either. Each view would incorrectly link Karla's overt behavior with an unconscious abhorrence of her femininity. Gender identity confusion and uncertainty of female body image were never in evidence in treatment. Rather, the use of the pen seemed to serve a more personal, self-fulfilling function as a soother, cementing her identification with this aspect of the therapist as an idealized selfobject as well as with his thoughtful analytic attitude. The activation of her symptom in the transference relationship amounted to a detoxification of the defensive elements that had led to earlier thefts from her mother and the acting out involving both her neighbor and her peers. The symptomatic theft of the pen thus favored mastery of her transference conflicts with a symbolized parent figure rather than an impulsive acting out that would only have served to perpetuate a pathological pattern.

The last of the self structures to arise, and unique to the consolidation of the nuclear self at the end of adolescence, are the internalizations of twinship or alterego experiences with peers and other adults external to the family of origin. The alterego pole reflects strivings for a sense of identity with others and membership in a group bound together in conformity to codes of behavior, values, goals, and life purpose. Kinship within this special circle of selfobjects attests to desires for likeness and similarity. Such strivings for a congruent identity with others, as alterego selfobject phenomena, were amply evident in each of Karla's thefts and underscored her wish for cementing, through her acting out, her perceived similarity to significant external others. Her fantasies of being the daughter of her neighbor served to differentiate her self from her maternal object of separation and simultaneously ally with an adult who shared the same fashion interests and related cultural worldviews. Of course, her unique spin on this selfobject expression of needs for inclusion in a twinship was that, to join in her group, her mother merely had to conform to being "hip" by adopting the mores of the current pop culture and thus identifying with her daughter rather than being Karla's object of identification.

In a similar vein, the fashionable clothes she shoplifted for her best friends' benefit, vicariously identifying through altruistic surrender, represented attempts to solidify her oneness with her peers, affirming shared identities as peers in a sisterhood. The thefts of clothing—the neighbor's and the store's—were symbolic statements of her selfobject needs that signified connection, differentiation, and likeness all at the same time. Contextualized in attachment and object relations terminologies, Karla performed holding environment functions for each member of her cohort as she enabled them to attach to her as a secure base, actively empathizing with their emotional turmoil while she vicariously revisited her own conflictual dyad experience with her mother. This kinship system expanded on the central themes of her developing identity—independent functioning, agency, affect regulation, impulse control, emerging character traits, and, paradoxically, pro-social behavior. These overlapping, multiple functions of a consolidating identity correspond to the neural processes located in the prefrontal orbital regions at the apex of the right hemisphere in the neocortex and in turn derive from their precursors in the unity of first attachments, separation, and affect regulation at the base in the brainstem and the amygdala (Cozolino, 2002). It is in these regards that "borrowing" my pen to write her final exams also served an alterego selfobject transference wish by identifying with her therapist in the mastery of knowledge as a prelude to her eventual success in future academics preparatory to choice of a career.

Reflecting on the meaning of Karla's immersion in the lives of her peers, from her estrangement from them to reunification with them, permitted a prolonged working through of her separation-individuation conflicts in large measure conditioned by my evolving construction of a working model of the mind of her mother as a symbiotic object for her daughter. Maintaining an "evenly suspended attention" to the multiple psychodynamics that were involved in virtually every one of her peer relations—Karla's separation anxieties, ambivalence in object relations, and all good/all bad self and object splits—stabilized the therapy by preventing me from prematurely interpreting her projective identification defenses. In particular, my reflective focus on her cycles of affect discharge—rage followed by wishes for repair and reunion—were repetitions that actually served adaptation and mastery as her integration of these emotional states and their regulation replaced a potential fixation point in her development. These therapeutic activities that operationalized a mindsight-oriented approach to understanding self, others, and interpersonal experience covered a vast mental territory that was at once emotionally implicit and repressed, verbally conscious and present-oriented, and defensive and adaptive. In this fashion, Karla's emerging stable states of attuned, loyal confidante to her friends in distress repeated her own early attachment history of multiply encoded, relational experiences of "feeling felt" within the maternal-infant holding environment. That I performed in this role, in the larger context of Karla's life, symbolically in the transference as a symbiotic source of emotional supply, confirmed her early separation arrest history and informed the treatment with subjective clinical data that could be validly retrieved in no other possible way.

Following my own clinicianly path of introspection led me backward in time to scan a conflict over an identification with a parent requiring forceful differentiation, one so very similar to Karla's. In so doing, I performed mental time travel to an experience in my own autobiographical past, a function of therapeutic "autonoetic consciousness" (Wheeler, Stuss, & Tulving, 1997, p. 333). The insight thus gained became the content, intersubjectively, to be shared via a personal self-revelation through informed technical activity. Purged of its solipsistic, cathartic, and aggrandizing potential, the inherent narcissism of that part self-idealized image was transcended for my client's benefit as one of the functions of vicarious introspection. The self-disclosing communication became empathic, not despite its narcissistic features, but because of them. The motivation was object-centered rather than self-centered and intuiting the proper timing of its utterance was critical. Had it remained an unspoken memory, or had it been incorporated into a fleeting countertransference reverie, or were it to have become the manifest content of a dream, its clinical usefulness, in the intersubjective context of a dual unity of therapeutic and adolescent selves in interaction would, at these moments, have been lost forever.

It is evident from the discussion of Karla's early history, most recent adolescent developmental stage, and an intersubjectivist approach to her treatment that multiple theories were required to understand her conflict and to engage her: drive theory, structural theory, a theory of ego autonomy, object relations theory, neurobiology, and self psychology. Each is a micro theory with clinically relevant metaphors. Because her symptoms of internal distress were rooted in her early history, the genetic point of view was never discarded.

While it may be that an understanding of arrests in the development of a cohesive self (Kohut, 1971) would best serve the goal of a dynamic assessment of this or any other adolescent client's level of functioning and personality development, the most useful application of self psychology principles arose in the context of the treatment relationship and therapeutic communication mode. That mode can be characterized as an interpersonal field of affective experiencing where the therapist attuned to the feelings of his client (D. N. Stern, 1985; Lichtenberg, 1989). The key feature of the intersubjective approach is the therapist's functioning as a bridge to connect his and the adolescent client's subjective worlds of experience. Such a linkage strengthens the adolescent's core sense of self and fosters its cohesion. The psychodynamic reconstruction of Karla's history, enabling her therapist to better understand her development, past and present, however, relied on a more traditional, ego psychology approach to behavior, object relations, and conflict formation. Neither approach to this adolescent, singly, would have eventuated in as productive a therapeutic venture.

Splitting and Identity Confusion

This section of chapter 3 presents a conceptual formulation, derived from developmental object relations theory and ego psychology, of the passage in male adolescence that culminates with the achievement of a masculine heterosexual identity. Themes of psychosexuality, male gender attributes, masculinity and object preference, and sexual orientation are discussed with reference to the adolescent stage. Finally, the critical tasks, core conflicts, and internalizations of prior developmental stages, especially with regard to the phases of the first separation-individuation process as well as the integration that is required of adolescence proper relative to a sexual identity as heterosexual and masculine, are highlighted through an extensive case illustration of an adolescent male with sexual identity confusion.

Unique to male adolescence is the integrative route to a mature, sexual body image. This developmental passage involves two distinct way stations. The first requires the normative regression to the archaic pre-oedipal mother and emancipation via a second individuation (Blos, 1965, 1967). In this formulation the pre- and early adolescent male re-experiences the anxieties of maternal engulfment and omnipotent overcontrol. Because the adolescent phases, psychosexually, focus on genitality, old fears of genital injury return from repression. In this regard, bisexuality concerns the reawakened awareness of gender differences and reflects, normatively, the potential for being less than completely male, that is, confused in his anatomical likeness to other males and his dissimilarity to females. Common to the fantasy life of male adolescents in these phases is wonderment at the qualities that define femaleness: procreation, gestation, birth and delivery, lactation, and the specific attributes that enable women to become mothers. As self-doubt gradually resolves, what is uniquely female is differentiated from what is anatomically male, and through projective identification, the ego alien elements—feminine and maternal gender characteristics—become the sole province, rightfully, of the opposite sex (Blos, 1962).

Passage through the first way station in early adolescent development is facilitated by a heightened identification with the father in the negative oedipal scenario. This involves an isogender (Blos, 1985), that is, a same-gender, libidinal attachment with wishes for sexual intimacy in relationship with the father and a corresponding bisexual confusion. Profound ambivalence may be expressed in aggressively tinged interactions with the mother. Displacements of the latter conflict are frequently observed in the young adolescent male's vituperation of female peers and insults aimed at thinly veiled, older adult authority figures (Lucente, 1986). The outcome of this conflict and its resolution is a further differentiation of male gender and, paradoxically, a deeper acceptance by the son for the mother of early childhood.

Masturbation in early adolescence fuels the fantasies of male bisexual conflict. Since the body in the masturbatory act is both subject as well as sexual part object, sexual expression lacks the finality of intercourse in that, in fantasy, any potential variant on one's developing sexual package can be center stage. Oral, anal, and phallic zones of stimulation may be coupled to masculine or feminine identifications that are tied to heterosexual, homosexual, or bisexual trends in object finding. Therefore, the issue of psychic structure is primarily anatomical in this first way station and involves the resolution of the adolescent male's bisexual identity confusion coupled to an acceptance of the female gender configuration as different in form, purpose, and function. When guided by a central masturbation fantasy that is heterosexually based (Laufer, 1968), the stage is set for entry into relationships that confirm one's masculine heterosexuality. While masturbation is an autoerotic, narcissistic pathway for sexual expression, it also paves the way for bisexual conflict resolution. The ultimate confirmation of intact maleness as the core gender attribute will await actual erotic experiences with females in adolescence proper. Falling in love with intimacy, romance, and sexual passion solidifies one's sexual makeup as does no other experience.

Consolidation of sexual identity, expressed both in object choice and in the behaviors that characterize an ideal, masculine self-image, is the core issue in adolescence proper (Blos, 1962). Falling in love in this critical stage prior to adulthood results in an experience wherein one's heterosexuality is mirrored through the eyes of the romantic partner (Erikson, 1968). Genitality is confirmed relative to organ mode, code of conduct involving loyalty to a significant other, and masculine behavior. What is inner and congruent corresponds to the sameness perceived by an affirming object. In this passionate relationship with a female peer, the male carries out an identification, likewise, with his mother. Relative to this maternal identification, object images that are female and ego alien are modified through the reinternalization of traits that become affiliated with the self (Schafer, 1968). Nurturance, expressiveness, affectivity, dependency strivings, and tenderness are integrated into one's masculine sexuality via a line of development in love relationships that repeats core elements from the first intimacy of infancy (Blanck & Blanck, 1986; Erikson, 1959, 1963; Gabbard, 2005; Lucente, 1994).

The internalizations that occupy center stage in the second way station prior to sexual identity consolidation are decidedly more complex than those in the first. Because they involve the various identificatory processes leading to an autonomous capacity for masculine sexuality versus being merely male in anatomy, a full interplay of object relations forces is at work in the second way station. De-identification with the femininity of the mother is achieved through a hyper-identification with the father of separation-individuation and the oedipal phase, that is, the isogender object relationship. However, significant interpersonal dilemmas involving insecurity in a male-bound attachment and a sense of inhibition, due to fear of competition with the father, confront every male child, not once but twice, prior to identity consolidation.

The potential pathology of an unresolved dyadic attachment to the father of separation would be a fusion with the paternal object: the inability to express oneself as independent in heterosexual relations, looking frantically to other males for confirmation of one's masculinity instead of to females. The selfsame anatomical invariant, the father-son template of shared gender that promoted the son's emancipation from the mother of symbiosis, carries with it an equally risky potential of isogender conflict, that is, fusion with the paternal object. In this regard, the toddler son might experience the father as either engulfing or rejecting. The resulting internalizations would be part-object representations based on traumatic frustration. The part-self representation, in interaction with such an object, would be internalized as inadequate and forever dependent on a superior male authority.

The affect state characterizing such an identificatory process would be based on overwhelming performance anxiety in heterosexual encounters. A son, unable to dissolve his bonds of attachment to an idealized father, would be inhibited and guilty in his search for heterosexual expression, not based on the oedipal fear of competition and subsequent paternal defeat through castration, but on an incapacity to risk his sexual identity in an intimate relationship modeling autonomous, masculine performance. In this formulation of conflict, there would be a noticeable lack of congruent, masculine imagery indicating an identification deficit due to isogender conflict with the dyadic father of separation-individuation.

While the adolescent boy seldom consciously doubts his maleness anatomically, sexual identity and heterosexual masculinity remain the subject of continuing uncertainty throughout the adolescent subphases. The mechanisms of incorporation, introjection, projective identification, identification with the aggressor, identification through altruistic surrender, and identification proper all promote the internal stability of object and self representations relative to the adolescent's sexual identity. These mechanisms variously serve defensive as well as adaptive purposes. Ultimately, they provide a foundation that supports a sense of oneself as masculine versus merely male. The residual clusters of object relations experiences, precipitates of abandoned object cathexes (S. Freud, 1923), become internalized islands of unambiguous, masculine certainty. These processes leading to heterosexual identity formation, including all adaptive/defensive internalizations of self in interaction with objects and the affective coloring of each successive encounter (Kernberg, 1976), terminate with a closure that signals passage through the stage of genitality into young adulthood.

Identification as transitory defense ends, therefore, where an active adult sexual identity begins (Erikson, 1968). An ego syntonic and secure sexual identity presumes that the adolescent was not exposed to massive physical or sexual abuse trauma, that psychosexual and psychosocial maturational processes were not imbued with overwhelming conflict, and that adequate peer reinforcements were available to heal the normative, unavoidable narcissistic scars of interpersonal familial experiences. Relative to intrapsychic structure, a stable masculine identity would hinge upon a self-representation structure that has become progressively more differentiated in maleness and is imbued with positive and aggrandizing affective memory traces of formative interpersonal experiences with idealized male authorities. Regarding identificatory processes, sexual self structure would be constituted from a minimum of ego alien, conflictual impingements of traumatizing objects in interaction with the self. An unconflicted heterosexual identity would, therefore, involve the internalizations of good object representations of one's father as well as imagery from other significant male authority figures. These representations would coexist, side by side, with a view of one's own evolved sexuality as autonomous, assertive, and independent, yet capable of mutuality. This evolved sexual identity, as both anatomically male and interpersonally masculine, would include the virtues of endurance in the face of conflict, rationality, objectivity, self-reliance, and competence. Capacities for warmth, caring, empathy, and tenderness augment the sexual identity package and probably owe their presence to the internalization of part object representations based on relationship intimacies with each parent but primarily with the mother.

To summarize, the elements of a heterosexual identity consist of anatomical reality, gender identity, intrapsychic structure (identifications and self and object representations), sexual orientation (female erotic object preference), and role enactments (culturally prescribed interpersonal behaviors). Relative to structure is the identificatory system that defines one's inner image as mature and sexually complete, like father, and a sexual self representation that is confirmed through the perceptions of significant others. Thus, object and self representations as a genital adult-to-be are constant and integrated into a congruent whole. The gender role enactments that are culturally prescribed ally with this inner structure to produce reasonably predictable interpersonal expressions vis-à-vis females. While unconsciously derived wishes from early childhood exist in all males for same-gender, sexual intimacy, there is a conscious awareness of preference for females and this attraction leads to arousal. The inherent complexity of male heterosexual identity consolidation in adolescence proper can be illustrated through clinical description. In the case summary that follows, the adolescent client presented with specific interpersonal sexual behaviors (orientation) that were incongruent with his overall sexual identity. He presented, initially, in a state of panic that threatened the fragile cohesion of his sexual identity. Feeling neither comfortable nor consciously safe in the company of female peers, he was, nevertheless, still amazed that he could be aroused homoerotically. In summary, sexual identity confusion was the precipitating crisis that led to treatment.

Tall, ruggedly handsome, and athletic, twenty-year-old Fred entered outpatient treatment at his own request after a brief psychiatric hospitalization. Observation had been required to avert a threatened but unspecified suicide attempt. The ostensible precipitant to his suicidal ideation, an acute bisexual panic which he was able to discuss haltingly and only with considerable difficulty, was the traumatic discovery of his sexual interest in his best male friend and roommate. The two had picked up a coed one Friday night at a local bar in the college town where all three resided as students, partied until closing time, and proceeded to the young men's apartment to engage in a group ménage à trois sexual encounter. Of paramount importance to the presenting problem, and of considerable diagnostic significance to understanding the context of Fred's acute crisis, was the older roommate's impending college graduation and acceptance of a job offer in a faraway state. The anxiety generated over both the acute event and the contributing loss of the relationship prevented Fred from maintaining full-time student status and, lacking the emotional resilience to continue as an emancipated teen, necessitated his returning to live with his family consisting of mother, father, and younger sister in the nearby community where he had been reared as a child.

The client also struggled with the relationship needs of his current girlfriend (older by three years) with whom he had had an ambivalent, "off and on" connection from his junior year in high school when they began dating. She was pressuring him for an engagement announcement and a ring. The more she demanded, the more he felt threatened. After sex with her, he would stand naked looking at himself in the mirror as if to reassure himself of his intactness and wholeness. These were experiences that contrasted sharply to his feelings of power and well-being when in close companionship with his roommate.

As an ancillary staff member with treatment privileges in the inpatient psychiatric unit, I was also able to conduct assessment interviews with his parents, also meeting briefly with his sister and the girlfriend who had facilitated his admission the night before. Investigating the sexual theme as part of the presenting problem, I elicited from him a sexological history involving first memories. As a young child he had witnessed primal-scene events on two separate occasions. His parents actively participated in a couples' bowling league and on Friday nights, after the competition, would party and bar hop, arriving home late, long after Fred was asleep. Awakened by a commotion downstairs, Fred would furtively tiptoe down the staircase, being careful lest he be caught and fearful of subsequent punishment, surreptitiously watching as his mother and father noisily copulated on the family room sofa. Later, as an early maturing adolescent (all pubertal sexual characteristics were fully developed by the age of thirteen), Fred depicted his first heterosexual experience, which occurred while he was in the eighth grade with a notoriously promiscuous seventeen-year-old, as being "seduced and abandoned." He remembered this encounter at the time as being overwhelming and confusing, with a mixture of anticipation, anxiety, guilt, and surprise cloaked in self-doubt. It was at this same time that Fred began substance use, experimenting first with alcohol and cannabis and then progressing to sporadic ingestion of hallucinogens.

Other important elements of his history included his popularity with peers, which was based significantly on his athleticism. Gifted with natural hand-eye coordination, extraordinary muscle mass and strength, ambidexterity, and flexibility, he avidly pursued baseball in Little League, frequently batting over .500. His coaches bragged that he was on base more often than not and had more RBIs than any other three players on the team summed together. This adulation from peers and selfobject mirroring from these significant authority figures in his life stood in stark contrast to his parents, his father in particular, who infrequently attended his games and offered neither praise nor encouragement. The notable exception to this coldness in the atmosphere of the family was his relationship with his paternal grandmother, who always attended his baseball games, idealizing and supporting her grandson and his prowess in all of his pursuits just as she had done ever since he could first remember, until her untimely death when he was ten.

Treatment hours in this initial stage consisted of (1) pursuing the presenting problem, that is, the sexual identity theme, potential drug involvement, and peer relations and girlfriend issues; (2) his plans for a future occupation and the college major that might support it; and (3) reflection on his relationships with the parents and with his sister for whom he had a special, affectionate bond. As he revealed more and more of the motive force behind this almost parental concern for her safety and well-being, it became possible to interpret and then to explore his fear that his sister would receive the same treatment from their mother and father that he had experienced: the inconsistent availability of his preoccupied mother due to her chronic dysthymia and moodiness, the angry tirades of his alcohol-abusing father on the weekends when he drank heavily, and the child neglect associated with a potential reoccurrence of sexual inappropriateness. As Fred engaged in this process of reflection and self-observation, demonstrating a commitment to the therapeutic alliance, he recalled early memories of angry arguments, usually in response to his failures to follow through with assigned household chores that often culminated in corporal punishment at the hands of both parents.

Pursuing the presenting problem in all of its forms ad infinitum cannot be overemphasized in this initial phase of therapy. My queries about his use of alcohol in the context of his acute crisis with the coed and his roommate led to further revelations about his drugs of choice; before leaving the bar all three had "dropped acid." The ensuing bad trip confirmed for Fred that LSD, at least for him, had serious, toxic potential and, even though he had experienced pleasurable euphoric states on other occasions, hallucinogens more frequently produced panic bordering on terror. Fred's sound reality-testing in this fashion permitted a psychoeducational approach, as well, to limit-setting on his use of alcohol. Focusing on his parents' background with their own history of abuse and the influence of their cultural belief system, which supported both solitary as well as barroom drinking, I was able to point to the research literature linking genetics and familial patterns to the transmission of addictive outcomes to offspring.

As these problem areas were more fully explored, Fred alluded to another concern, the unreliable and exploitive, asocial pseudo-friends with whom he had become increasingly involved lately in procuring and using cannabis. Eventually, I was able to employ an interpretive strategy to connect his acting out of self-destructive impulses, camouflaged by his drug use, to his pattern of avoiding the tensions in his separation difficulties with his parents, and partialize his defensive identification with the aggressor (i.e., his father), as a consequence of his earlier oedipal-phase trauma. However, a preparatory foundation for this working through, which occurred at a much later stage in his treatment, involved the clarification of the impact of his primal-scene exposure at the age of six. As Fred remembered the event as bewildering, overwhelming, and guilt producing, I remarked on the natural curiosity of oedipal children in their fantasies of the private sex lives of parents, making a matter-of-fact observation that these are universal features of the relationships of sons and mothers and fathers and daughters. I also clarified that what had occurred in Fred's sixth year of life was more the opposite, that is, that the reality of the actual deeds had instead intruded on his fantasies. How could it have been anything other than overwhelming in light of his age and the fact that he had not been protected from exposure to the sexual act, which was supposed to have been private instead of public? Finally, I pointed out to Fred that his normal fantasies of a three-person system, involving both conflict and seduction and dovetailing with the primal-scene exposure comprising the same triad, seemed inseparable from the acute recent crisis that had also involved three persons: all three sexual experiences involved two males and a single female.

In this early stage of his treatment, all-or-none, highly ambivalent discussions of his college career and areas of occupational interest predominated, revealing an identity diffuseness that would eventually come to characterize much of the middle phase of treatment. As one area was devalued, another would be idealized, and I found myself gradually being related to accordingly (i.e., as either an all-good or all-bad therapist). His occupational strivings were diametric and twofold. He had chosen art as his initial major and reveled in the creative geniuses of the great masters. On the other hand, he described states of total immersion in his own artistic endeavors that left him feeling fragmented and weak: commissioned by his aunt and uncle to paint an elaborate, art deco mural on their garage door, he consumed art book after art book in the planning and design phase, finally spending as many as sixteen hours a day on its completion. Subsequently, when he changed his major to engineering, it was because he felt compelled to pursue a more practical and virile profession rather than one dominated by role models who lacked discipline and rationality.

As Fred described his three-year, sporadic relationship with his girlfriend, it soon became apparent that Joan represented a powerful protector female, an all-forgiving and accepting maternal object, but one who was now demanding an intimacy that threatened him with loss of cohesion, splitting his self-representations into molar images of male-female, strong-weak, and potent-emasculated. When her sexual drive and interests were less intense, he felt gratified and rewarded for his complementary solicitous, paternal behavior toward her. While the relationship appeared to be evolving and maturing with more stable patterns of communication and more reasonable expectations of the other, Fred remained unable to self-observe, reflect on, and predict his emotional responses to her from one day to the next, and there still remained instances of abrupt breakups triggered by seemingly trivial occurrences.

As he revealed more of this fertile relationship material in the initial stage of treatment, he described an event from the evening before. The two had dined at a fancy restaurant with their friends and as he spoke, he became increasingly anxious and almost dissociative as his eyes glazed over. He had relied on Joan to choose the restaurant, make the reservations, converse with their friends at the table, and to take the lead in general. Sensing his anxiety, Joan began to consume glass after glass of wine, becoming increasingly giddy and childlike, and eventually excused herself to find the restroom. Ten minutes later she was retrieved by the maitre d', who had found her lost and stumbling in the kitchen area, and was escorted back to the table. Fred's mounting anxiety in the office over the course of this replay of events quickly changed to embarrassment and then to unbridled fury. In subsequent treatment hours he described his mortification and contempt for this child figure who had previously represented the pinnacle of tact, adult self-control, and maternal omnipotence. In short, he now felt compelled to reject her much as he had experienced ejection from the symbiotic orbit, the "dual unity" (Mahler et al., 1975) of her holding and protection.

As Fred proceeded with these themes in his relationship with Joan—ambivalent strivings and defensive splitting, denial and predominantly projective identification mechanisms, and the various and sundry reenactments of his separation-individuation history from passive to active—I found myself unconsciously identifying with the hurt and anguish of Joan and her unfair treatment at the hands of her boyfriend and my client. At this juncture, Fred's attack on Joan suddenly shifted to a full-scale verbal assault on me, now demanding that I commence a long-term psychotherapy of his fiancée-to-be, with the aim of treating her regression so that she might return to normal adult functioning, that is, to restore her to her proper role as his rewarding maternal provider to complement his split self-image as the emasculated toddler. Unaware of my loss of the direction of the therapy—of pace, interventions, focus, patience, and patient—I abruptly refused. Instead, I interpreted to Fred my understanding of his unconscious wish to keep separate and unmetabolized his own dual images of the haughty, punitive parent to the needy, anxious child inside himself. The result of these interventions was spectacular. Sensing my fear of fragmenting the professional self into its two extremes, the archaic split-part images of childlike playfulness and professional austerity, Fred voiced his reluctance to continue in individual treatment with me and demanded a referral to a couples' counselor specializing in premarital work. In effect, just as Fred had experienced a lack of understanding from Joan who became inebriated and regressed in the restaurant, as his therapist I had also reacted unempathically by becoming rigid and unapproachable as if hiding from him behind my identification with Joan and my interpretations of his unconscious conflicts. In each instance, a superior, omnipotent object was required to intervene: the maitre d' in the first instance, to rescue Joan from herself, and a specialist from a more established discipline, psychology, to prevent me from continuing in my failure to recognize and comprehend the depth of his emotional pain and turmoil. Although a premature termination was averted and an empathic re-alliance was established based on my awareness of the abandonment threats he re-experienced in his relationship with his significant other and with me, nevertheless, the themes of differentiation and the projective identification defenses that served to perpetuate an unintegrated self and object constancy continued to pervade the transference relationship.

Fred's middle phase of therapy slowly evolved as the transference relationship became less volatile. Interpretation of his projective identifications and displacements of his separation-individuation conflicts with his mother were facilitated by a therapeutic strategy of mentalizing his relationship reenactments with Joan. Describing his girlfriend as driven to become a mother as the single most salient feature of her adult, feminine identity, he self-reflected on his own needs to be treated by her as her son. He speculated that his evolving relationship needs for mutuality and interdependence were at odds with her motivation to parent him and thereby to perpetuate his dependency on her as a small child. As he replayed in a number of sessions the arguments with her that ensued after he vowed to sign up for intramural athletics at the university with plans to commit to baseball and hockey, I invited him to speculate on ". . . whatever could she have had in mind?" in opposing his interest in these team sports. Reflecting on her mindsightedness, in interaction with his increasing self-agency, yielded insights into her jealousy of his appropriate peer attachments and her insecurity in losing him to sports. On another level, and relative to his sexual relationship with Joan, it became apparent that it lacked the passion and intensity that characterize romantic partners, and, with some appropriate expressions of guilt, Fred came to the conclusion that his impulsive infidelity with the coed was but another defensive acting out of his issues with emancipating from Joan and separating from the dyadic, maternal bond from early childhood.

Fred's individuation and further de-identification with his maternal object returned him to the normative, phase-appropriate progression to attaining a heterosexual sense of self. Consolidation of sexual identity in the adolescent male requires a resolution of the same-gender, libidinal attachment to the father of the first oedipal phase coupled with a differentiation from this paternal object representation at the same time (Lucente, 1996; Blos, 1985; S. Freud, 1924). This twofold, complex task for Fred signified a potential fixation point in bisexual identity confusion, fostered in large measure by his ambivalent attachment to and distancing from his relationship with an emotionally unavailable father. As transference repeated development (Basch, 1980), Fred opened the door to a deeper, more connected relationship with me, and the quality of the transference relationship changed significantly. I found myself becoming the idealized, masculine selfobject for whom he had been searching in his formative latency years. In a fashion similar to the mentalizing interventions that enabled Fred to understand the complex issues of his separation-individuation conflicts, which he symbolically displaced and acted out repetitively with me in the transference and with Joan, the transferred wishes and fears vis-à-vis his father became subject to reflection and scrutiny as well. He described his father as alexithymic, uninterested, and at the same time seemingly unaware of emotions in self and others. As he came to know the mind of his father, Fred recounted the stories of his father's life growing up on the "mean streets" of the inner city in a tough, ethnic neighborhood where the code of honor and expected behaviors included fistfights, after school and in the alleyways, to resolve differences when more polite, verbal combat produced stalemates. Toughness on the one hand, and sharing feelings on the other, were at opposite ends of the spectrum in this code of male behaviors where the former reflected the ideal and the latter its absence. Fred's reflections on the current state of affairs with his father produced more insight into the reasons for the high expectations his father had for him as well as the son's own adoption of his father's code of expectations for himself. Furthering mindsight into these aspects of self and other and performing "mental time travel" (D. J. Siegel, 1999) back in time to his father's early history, his attitude toward him softened considerably as he came to understand these high expectations as defensive maneuvers designed to ward off the father's fears of failure as well as to guard against his defeat in a hostile environment.

Concomitant with these revelations and insights into the paternal relationship, Fred's father consulted with the human resources department where he worked and was given a referral to a twelve-step program, which he accepted, albeit under duress. While the subsequent abstinence contract was non-negotiable, nevertheless it was followed, much to the delight of all family members, by the formerly hostile and withdrawn husband and father becoming more approachable and responsive to the needs of spouse and children. This was a serendipitous outcome in the course of Fred's psychotherapy, but oftentimes we as clinicians tend to underestimate the profound impact on family members and their own subsequent potentials for change that result from the identified client's progress in treatment.

Reflection on these changes in the temper and quality of his relationship with his father continued to occupy considerable therapy time. Retrieving the sequence of events from his early latency years, formerly forgotten, that led to his immersion in baseball and Little League, Fred recollected a typical weekday evening. After dinner, night after night, his fatigued father would routinely don the baseball glove, bat, and hardball to practice with his son the basics of the game: hitting and pepper, assuming the proper stance at the plate, and the proper choke on the bat. These memories included his father's infectious enthusiasm for the game, the gracious introduction of his son to the coaches in the Little League system, and his active presence with Fred during team tryouts. Naturally perplexed at the disparity between this version of his father and the previous portrayal of him as emotionally unavailable, I wondered out loud what Fred thought about what I might be thinking. Intuiting the same contradiction, Fred responded by recounting a recent conversation with his father on the same subject. His father had withdrawn from the Little League scene due to the pressure he sensed from the other teammates' parents to appropriate their sons' experiences, making them their own, and also because the coaching staff had become more insistent that he increase his time spent with managing the team and recruiting during the off-season, an availability to which he simply could not commit. Reflecting on this new information and in the context of an evolving working model of his father's mind in simultaneous interaction with the mind of the seven-year-old son, Fred's sense of being his father's son—valued, esteemed, and similar—also included the emerging, prideful respect for a parent whose motivation to absent himself from the game he loved was predicated on the altruistic wish to not contaminate or otherwise jeopardize his son's future with the sport of baseball.

As I pondered the ease with which Fred had availed himself of the therapeutic alliance—as an invitation to reflect on his subjective past and its constructed multiple meanings—he asked if he had ever mentioned his childhood relationship with his paternal grandmother. In subsequent treatment hours there emerged a narrative of her generosity—of the quality time spent with her grandson, while two busy working parents were consumed with making ends meet, as she provided the selfobject functions of affirming, mirroring, soothing, and idealizing. It was Gramma who attended school functions, both with him and on his behalf at parent-teacher conferences; it was Gramma who tirelessly read and reread her grandson's favorite stories at bedtime; it was Gramma who always let him win at checkers and who learned the computer software games they shared together on so many afternoons after school; it was Gramma who drove him to the hospital emergency room when he broke his finger sliding into home plate

during a baseball game. And it was Gramma whose untreated high blood pressure led to a series of debilitating cerebrovascular accidents that eventually
necessitated her removal from her home of forty years, to which she never returned, and to permanent residence in a nursing home. Fred's poignant retelling
of the final six months with his beloved grandmother began with her gradual
loss of anterograde memory followed quickly by declines in organ systems that
necessitated 24-hour, skilled care. It was during the second to the last visit with
her in the nursing home, after he had given her a box of her favorite chocolates,
that he realized she no longer recognized him. In his last visit with her, three
months before she expired, he noticed with dismay that the box of chocolates
had been opened but that only half of a single candy had been consumed, with
the remainder in a state of moldy decay. Fred never saw her again nor did he
grieve at her funeral; it was as if she had died many months before when she no
longer recognized him. During these sessions Fred wept copious tears, intermit-
tently, as he remained active in his grief, verbalizing his sadness, and eventually
saying goodbye. Fred's grief work signaled the beginning of his termination after
eighteen months of individual psychotherapy.

Working through for Fred was evident in his resolution of the separation-
individuation conflicts, involving both parents, and their thinly veiled reenactments in virtually every one of his other interpersonal relationships. As a consequence of this progress, relationships with both parents had improved considerably and were more adult-like, indicating little potential for a regressive return
to his formerly rebellious, acting out, and ultimately self-defeating behaviors.
Coupled with his increased capacities for reality testing, introspection, and
empathy, his other relationships also benefited, for example, with peers and with
his sister, who resumed her proper role in a brother's object relations with a sibling versus being a target for his projective identifications. While the quality of
communication had improved with Joan, once he reached an understanding of
her needs to infantilize him that only compounded his own dependency conflicts, the relationship gradually faded away, without fanfare or dramatics.

Numerous other factors militated in support of termination. Fred's peer involvements had gradually shifted from the asocial network of drug users to
friendships within the culture of his engineering major. Dating, which had
abruptly come to a standstill after his breakup, resumed, and his experiences
with the opposite sex seemed more reality based, less artificial and idealizing,
and more empathic. These appropriate experiences with erotic objects pointed

to a resolution of his castration anxiety and bisexual conflicts, suggesting an oedipal, masculine identification with his father. None of these current relationships had the flavor of all-or-nothing aggrandizements and devaluations so characteristic of his entanglement with Joan. Choice of career seemed eminently reasonable and had been thoroughly researched and indicated self-agency and effectance (White, 1963; D. N. Stern, 1985). While he remained intense in his engineering studies and passionate as he pursued "extra credit" for optional homework exercises, for example, solving advanced integral calculus equations and prove-ups that kept him studying well past midnight, none of these activities left him depleted or emotionally deflated as had his art projects. Finally, his reinvolvement in baseball, and athletics in general, indicated a purposeful return to the activities of past mastery that would continue to enhance his self-confidence, solidifying a mature identification with his father and providing a social forum for drive gratifications. The therapeutic termination decision was mutual and gradual over a two-month period, and included the "open door" invitation to return in the future if necessary.

Reflections on the Treatment Process

Fred's treatment commenced with an identity crisis of panic proportions, paradoxically permitting a smooth and natural process of engagement from the very outset wherein I provided a "secure base" for the entire course of therapy. This secure base (Bowlby, 1969; Main & Solomon, 1986), or holding environment (Winnicott, 1960b), permitted an empathic attunement (Atwood & Stolorow, 1999) to Fred's central problems of attachment and the related second separation-individuation phase of adolescence. In object relations terms, therapy reopened the door to integrating and restructuring internalized object and self representations in the therapeutic relationship. Much of the change process transpired at an unconscious level: through the mechanism of projective identification, Fred's unconscious affect states of separation anxiety, depression, and rage and my own nonconscious acceptance of them joined together in the treatment relationship. This process of unconscious engagement commenced only hours after his admission when I met him for the first time after his breakfast on the ward as we walked to the interview office; the nonverbal connection was immediate and soothing, regulating, nonjudgmental, and empathic in large measure mediated by my gaze, physical presence and posture, attitude, facial expression, and tone of voice, and by my responses to his verbal and nonverbal cues.

In retrospect, the transference storms that occurred in the third month of treatment reactivated a deeply ingrained pattern of rapprochement phase (Mahler et al., 1975) misalliances and mirroring failures from the first separation experiences of the toddler phase. Expectations of being rejected, misunderstood, and shamed all converged with my countertransference rupture when I unwittingly overidentified with his girlfriend in the scene at the restaurant. Later, reflecting on this re-enactment with my countertransference feelings in sharp focus, I noted that in the weeks preceding Fred's threatened termination session, I had begun to prepare myself unconsciously for the eventual emotional assault as I psychobiologically attuned to his escalating anger (i.e., to the "moment-by-moment . . . rhythmic crescendos and decrescendos" of his autonomic nervous system as it resonated with my own felt sense of danger [A. N. Schore, 2003, p. 82]). Indeed, through my reflective self-focus, I became aware of the gradually increasing tension in my abdominal wall almost as if I were a boxer defensively preparing for a punch to the solar plexus. This mirroring response, at an unconscious, shared right hemispheric processing level of visceral affect, corresponds to D. J. Siegel's (2007) sixth sense of intuition and implicit emotional knowledge.

Suggestive of an underlying borderline personality organization, these projective identification mechanisms involved Fred's projection of toxic rage at the rejecting objects (parents, Joan, and myself) and a complementary and simultaneous purging of his painful part self-representation. In this intersubjectivist, affect-regulating treatment approach, and maintaining an "evenly suspended attention" (S. Freud, 1912b) to the ebbs and flows of Fred's multilevel communications, clinician and client paired in a reciprocal invitation from one unconscious mind to another to engage in a shared state of affect attunement. Partaking of the three subjectivities of "the analytic third" (Ogden, 1994)—clinician self, client self, and the shared illusory orbit in between—the mentalizing interventions with these projective identification mechanisms in the middle phase of therapy altered the manner in which self and object images, and their attendant affect states, were represented in Fred's implicit memory system. In this manner, therapeutic empathy detoxified the raw affects, which were then re-internalized by the client in a more benign, metabolized, and de-aggressivized representational form. As A. N. Schore (2003) points out, these reenactments are sudden and dramatic, but once addressed and worked through, they pave the way for significant positive changes through exploration and interpretation. The character changes that occurred have a neurobiological substrate, the result of alterations in the neural networks of the brain's right hemisphere as it appraised, processed, and encoded these conflictual affect states in new ways. Although emotion is infused throughout the entire brain, it was the affect centers in the cerebral right hemisphere that responded to the psychotherapeutic approach, that is, from the sensory-somatic, "lower brain areas"—the brain stem, limbic system, and amygdala—to the prefrontal orbitocortex at the "top" (A. N. Schore, 2003; Fonagy et al., 2002; D. J. Siegel, 1999). Therefore, while the semantic-based communication skills of the therapist represented the verbal workings of his conscious mind in the left hemisphere, it was the simultaneous engagement of the bilateral right hemisphere, from therapist to client and from client to therapist, that accounted for the effectiveness of the interpretive process. Finally, from the neurobiological point of view relative to the left hemisphere, the "word" itself is highly overrated and pales in comparison to the power and significance of the clinician's underlying affect, tone of voice, body posture, facial display and gaze, and all of the inert, but enduring, unique features of his personality that inform diction and word choice.

The mentalizing techniques in Fred's therapy that promoted improved affect regulation, self-awareness, and better mindsight into self and others were able to reach the basic fault (Balint, 1968) in his self system, that is, misalliances and attunement ruptures, reflective of his early maternal object of separation-individuation, and with the paternal object of identification in the second oedipal revision in adolescence. In regard to his improved relationship with his father, Fred's evolving capacity for mindsight was conditioned on his developing affect regulation involving self and others as he came to respect his intuitions and "gut hunches," reflect on them, and employ them to understand his relationships in deeper and more complex ways, that is, the sixth sense unconscious processing of emotional data (D. J. Siegel, 2007). Following the research of Fonagy and colleagues, "only when psychotherapy generates mentalized affectivity will this fault line in the psychological self be bridged" (2002, p. 11).

Although no psychotherapy is ever complete, fully addressing and resolving all areas of dysfunction, Fred's treatment enabled him to resume the developmental timetable at the stage-appropriate next level, that is, the dual tasks of young adulthood involving intimacy versus isolation and occupation (Erikson, 1963). In the latter regard, he evidenced agency and problem-solving skills that would augur well for success in the workplace. It is in the former regard that some concern still lingers. As he constructed his relationship with Joan from its beginning to its gradual fading away, I never sensed that he had fully been able to appreciate her, empathizing with her emotional complexity and with the multiplicity of her feelings for him. In sum, she had fulfilled an inner need for him as a transitional object, re-creating an in-between orbit of illusion between self and object where he was able to repair a misalliance rupture, re-internalizing in a form that would foster growth, without her, in new relationships with other women. I remain impressed by how much he had identified with her: his capacities for nurturance, tenderness, and mature interdependencies on others can all be attributed to her significance in his life. That he planned to continue with his interest in art, as an avocation, probably attests to her active presence, as an object representation, in his identity. With this single caveat in mind, however, this twenty-year-old is now on the way to object and self constancy, on the way to regulating affects, and on the way to consolidating identity as he embarks on the rest of the journey through adulthood.

Affect Regulation and the True Self

The continuing revisions of personality theory, made possible by the integration of recent research findings from studies of infants and young children, have had considerable impact on the way clinicians think about development as well as on the understanding that informs a psychodynamic assessment. The benefit to theory development has been the retention of significant elements of the older models, when juxtaposed with these new insights and conceptualizations, that both frame and delimit their roles. A major thrust of this chapter is to continue to explore the relationship between the concepts of adolescent identity formation, the second separation-individuation process, and the emerging paradigm, in contemporary psychoanalysis, informed by a theory of intersubjectivity. Exploring the concept of affect regulation, as a central feature of personality consolidation in the adolescent phase, constitutes a second thrust. Finally, after a review of theory and research, a case-focused discussion of two adolescent clients follows, highlighting the therapeutic process and the use of metaphorical language in treating these clients.

The capacity for regulating feelings, that is, constructing a personal meaning system based on an emotionally and affectively attuned ability to comprehend both self and others, bridges new and older theory. Affectivity also provides a linkage from normative developmental processes to clinical conditions and their treatment. This is so because the importance, clinically, of affective life, feeling states, and emotional tone is implicit throughout all of the psychodynamically oriented theories of personality. Furthermore, the complexity of internal, affective life can never be overestimated as a core assumption in psychotherapy. Because emotion is central to all aspects of the biopsychosocial field, affective experiences have meanings that span the intrapsychic and the internal, interpersonal, familial, cultural, and therapeutic contexts of human experience.

As a synthesizing agent crucial to personality formation, affect regulation is a psychodynamic developmental process that integrates the internal, intermediate, and externally objective experiences that form the foundation of one's unique autobiography. In the phasic and sequential construction of the overall personality, affect regulation also provides a conceptual basis for integrating compatible elements of ego psychology and object relations theory. Exploring the vicissitudes of two universal features of the adolescent phase, that is, identity formation and the related processes of separation and individuation, will highlight this union of ego psychology and object relations theory.

No longer compartmentalized as separate and isolated, affective life is now understood as unitary with cognition, language, perception, and behavior (Fonagy et al., 2002; Lackoff, 1987; A. N. Schore, 1994). Because the expression of affect is observable in neonates, some theorize that affects are innate (Emde, 1980). On the other hand, because certain complex affect states seem to be linked to developmental stages (e.g., oedipal guilt, eight-month stranger anxiety, and the Kleinian depressive position), affects also appear to be acquired. It would seem, therefore, that while emotional life is a constitutional given at birth, the affective sphere becomes increasingly elaborated, differentiated, and eventually integrated as the individual matures within a biopsychosocial field. In describing the relationship between biology and genetics, on the one hand, and early developmental experiences on the other, the former hold critical psychosocial constructions on a leash, but the tethering rope is both long and quite elastic.

From birth, infants perceive, emote, and encode their cognitions, as the psyche establishes a rudimentary organization for the internal representation of experiences, only some of which can be recalled from memory (D. J. Siegel, 1999). This structuring of infant affective experience occurs within the maternal holding environment and involves excitement and arousal as well as the regulation of emotional intensity (Winnicott, 1960b). The holding environment includes the facilitating, intermediate realm between the infant subject and the maternal object where the infant both creates and re-creates his own version of their intersubjective experiences. The infant's construction of emotionality includes both an awareness of affects as well as the range of feelings within discrete affect states, for example, the rising and falling of pleasure, sadness, or rage as the infant interacts with his maternal object (D. N. Stern, 1985). Adequate, "good enough" structuring, contingent upon maternal empathy, is eventually internalized and includes the subjective, somatic/visceral changes (both constitutional and biological) that always accompany genuine emotional states. While global affect states typify this early infant phase (pleasure, pain, organismic panic and fear of object loss, etc.), the young child will eventually differentiate sufficiently as a separating self with a more discriminating capacity for sensory awareness, affect expression, recognition of mood, and affect tolerance (Brown, 1993). Crucial to a successful passage through the adolescent stage is a further refinement of affect regulation, which is the last of these capacities to develop.

These features of early affect development have neurobiological, constitutional, genetic, and social components. The first group includes predictable, reflexive infant facial displays for experiencing discretely different feeling states: the eight primary response patterns, identified in Tomkins's research, of interest-excitement, enjoyment-joy, surprise-startle, distress, anguish, fear-terror, shame-humiliation, contempt-disgust, and anger-rage (1962, 1963). Second come the arousal processes (hyper, midrange, and hypo; D. J. Siegel, 1999), including the infant's construction of feelings in the maternal holding environment, particularly involving hearing and sight such as the matching of the mother's face with the infant's joy, fear, anxiety, or comfort/discomfort experiences, as well as attunements through the tempo and rhythm of the mother's voice (D. N. Stern, 1985; Beebe & Lachman, 1988). Third are the receptive awareness states of alert inactivity and curiosity, and the *in statu nascendi* self-observational capacity (forerunner of a secondary autonomy in Hartmann's sense of ego adaptation in the conflict-free sphere, 1939) that will eventually lead to signal anxiety functioning in anticipating, responding to, and expressing moods including characteristic negative affects, for example, eight-month stranger anxiety (Mahler et al., 1975; Tolpin, 1971). By the end of the first year of childhood, the stage is set for the development of *primary emotional experience* (Brown, 1993).

Affect Regulation: Primary and Secondary Emotional Experience

Defined as the initial ability to self-manage one's mood, *primary emotional experience* emerges from intersubjective episodes in the shared intermediate space, the illusionistic realm of creative construction, with the environmental mother accurately perceiving the infant's feelings in her mirroring function and transmitting this awareness through her ministrations (Winnicott, 1967b). This formative subjective self (validated as a feeling self), when the empathic mother reliably presents to her infant her own, inner object representation of him, is well prepared for the expanding potential for meaningful interpersonal encounters throughout life. These potentials, in future relationships of all kinds, spring from the infant's multiple experiences of "feeling felt" by his maternal object (D. J. Siegel, 1999).

However, in the absence of such a facilitating intermediate realm of experiencing, or more typically, where inconsistent, unreliable mothering occurs or where misalignments with mirroring failures are frequent, the separating toddler, never having "found" himself in his mother's mentalized object representation, internalizes, instead, the actual "real" external, mother object representation, replete with all of the misattunements and inconsistencies that characterized her unempathic behavior with her infant (Winnicott, 1967a; D. N. Stern, 1985; Atwood, Stolorow, & Trop, 1989). This rupture, which is defensively internalized through introjection as ego alien and part of the false self, remains essentially unconscious as a core deficit within the self system and may become the basis for later repetition-compulsion enactments from passive to active, interpersonally and intersubjectively, as a pathological consequence (Winnicott, 1960a). Saddled with significant impairments to the reflective and self-observing functions, the toddler then fails to develop self-knowledge and a capacity for knowing the minds of others through reconstructing his own as well as others' inner experience (Fonagy et al., 2002). He is thus doubly deprived, prone to the use of projective identification defenses and more likely to misattribute his own volitions, motivations, and conflictual feelings to others. Of greatest significance, however, is impairment of the capacity for *primary emotional experience*. The evolutionary history behind these concepts, derived from both infant observational research and metapsychological theorizing, involves a detailed accounting and is well beyond the scope of this chapter. However, for more details on that history, see the following: S. Freud, 1905a, 1911a, 1926; D. N. Stern, 1985; Main & Solomon, 1986; Jacobson, 1964; Spitz, 1965; Bowlby, 1969; Sullivan, 1953.

Formulations and revisions of the various regulatory mechanisms that arise to add stability, coherence, and structure to the developing infant personality have been legion in the history of psychoanalytic theorizing. Beginning of course with Freud's treatises on the pleasure-pain, reality, and nirvana principles and the repetition compulsion, these primary regulations function to govern the delay and control of the immediate discharge of aggressive and libidinal drives, ensure that secondary process thought and logic subordinate (but do not replace) primary process thinking and magical wish fulfillment, and provide a template for the internalization of trauma and conflict (S. Freud, 1911a, 1920, 1923).

Affirming Hartmann's suggestion (1939) that enhanced resilience proceeds from conflict resolution, in this latter regard Russell has attributed a synthetic function to the tendency to repeat the past, that is, the repetition-compulsion, as a universal feature of the human condition: "repetition is unavoidable, life proceeds by repetition . . . people come to understand their past not simply by . . . remembering . . . apparently, only through reliving the past can there come some kind of understanding that makes a difference" (1998, p. 1). The role that affect regulation plays in the mastery of past experience is central and ensures that emotions will serve the individual's goals of adaptation rather than entropy.

What follows is an enumeration of the various components of the affect regulation function, some recent literature that describes affect regulation processes, and an initial attempt at integrating elements of psychodynamic theory with findings from neurobiological research and constructivism. In early infancy, and prior to the structuralizing of the hippocampus and the prefrontal orbitocortex regions of the brain in the second and third years of life, the implicit memory system encodes patterns of feeling states primarily, but not exclusively, linked to relationships with the parents of attachment. It is in the limbic system, and more specifically within the amygdala, that the holding environment becomes represented internally as neural circuits develop through countless wirings of engrams of emotionally laden experience. These neural networks are not random: current experiences are encoded on the basis of past wirings, precluding the development of some neural networks, "pruning" them in favor of others. What fires together wires together (Hebb, 1949). The associational linkages, that is, internalized representations, are therefore the probabilities that future emotions will be stored and retrieved in similar ways. These earliest infant emotional experiences and their representations, the feelings "laid down" in the brain, are the primary emotions that characterize the processes of arousal, appraisal, and activation (D. J. Siegel, 1999). These primary emotions are the precursors to the categorical affects that will eventually emerge in the emotional repertoire of the older child who narrates experience through language use, retrieves episodes of remembered experience, and subjects them to verbalization, all of which define the processes more central to secondary emotional experience.

Prior to this, however, affect development in the first eighteen months is limited to the irretrievable, but permanently stored and encoded, implicit memories of the primary emotions. These primary emotions are constitutional, automatic, tension-inducing or reducing, stimuli-based, and frequently out of conscious awareness. The primary emotions represent the fundamental processes of emotional/visceral sensation. These emotions become internally represented in the implicit memory system and include hedonic tone in the mother-infant cultural field; the vitality-affect states, which demonstrate excitement, satiation, bodily comfort and discomfort; and the variations in libidinal lust/unlust gratifications, that is, pleasure and pain. These earliest relationship experiences, which cannot be retrieved with words, remain permanently encoded, continue to exert a profound influence on later attachments, and precondition individuals to a pattern of future expectations of others. These internalizations, and their subsequent wordless representations, have been described as islands of "unformulated experience" (D. B. Stern, 1983), and they contribute significantly to the interpersonal dynamics and operations of procedural memory (Lyons-Ruth, 1999). While the amygdala in the limbic system is the site for these early, emotion-laden engrams of infant experience with the environmental mother, the later development of the prefrontal orbito cortex, explicit memory, and the asymmetric, left hemisphere processing of events (digital, linear, logical, and language-based) is contingent on the quality of this earliest attachment relationship through affect attunement (A. N. Schore, 1994; D. J. Siegel, 1999) and affect resonance (Trevarthen, 1993, 1996).

In its broadest sense as a conceptual umbrella for the infant stage, the holding environment includes such related phenomena as maternal empathy, accurate attunement and affect mirroring, the ordinarily devoted mother and maternal preoccupation, transitional phenomena in the intermediate world of illusion, the subjective object and intersubjectivity, and gradual interdependence (Winnicott, 1951, 1956, 1960b, 1967b). These processes describe the pathway whereby affective life becomes differentiated and organized for the ongoing maturation of *primary emotional experience* during the later stages of childhood. In addition to the other developmental tasks of adolescence, profound changes occur in the teen's capacity to both experience and understand a greater range and depth of feeling. By the end of adolescence and at the brink of young adulthood, the individual will have a developmental base for *secondary emotional experience,* deriving from an evolved capacity for affect regulation. This higher-order capacity for regulating affect states involves a more sensitive awareness of the visceral and somatic signs that accompany feelings with an integration of these changes into an adultomorphic "body ego" that replaces that of the non-procreative child image of latency. For instance, the emotional experiences of arousal that accompany the adolescent's newfound sexuality will be encoded, neurobiologically, in a very different manner than previously. In addition, greater affect awareness and affect tolerance will also aid in selecting coping mechanisms to adaptively manage encounters in difficult interpersonal situations, such as conflicts with family members, authority figures, and peers.

Because the adolescent stage witnesses an entire revision of intellectual abilities related to abstract, reflective thought far beyond concrete operations and simple causality (the cognitive capacities for formal operations, hypothetico-deductive reasoning, mature judgment, and problem analysis; Piaget, 1950), subjective experiences now become the object of both scrutiny and retrospection. As the adolescent cognitively processes a feeling state (for instance anger), it may be compared and contrasted to previous experiences, communicated more satisfactorily and purposefully, understood as serving as a defense against other feelings, or it may trigger the taking of direct action. In any event, affect regulation presumes, first, that a fuller repertoire of feelings now exists, with nuances and gradations of meaning that can be reflected on. It also presumes that the adolescent is able to remain in an affect state and attend to it simultaneously. Doing so provides a partializing experience, as feelings are both differentiated and examined and then reintegrated into a new whole: reversibility of affective life is, of course, contingent on the reversibility function provided by formal operations and abstract reflective thought (Piaget, 1950). In summary, affect regulation consists of all processes responsible for understanding, monitoring, evaluating, and modifying one's emotions within a complex biopsychosocial field (Thompson, 1994). For the adolescent, attaining this higher level of affect regulation provides the basis for *secondary emotional experience*, ensuring that feelings will be processed in ever expanding and more complex ways; thus, "mentalization . . . brings about a new kind of interest in one's own mind" (Fonagy et al., 2002, p. 95).

Progressing to this higher level of affect regulation at the end of adolescence is a significant achievement in object relations terms. Self-reflecting on one's own emotional states now includes the ability to reflect on the subjective feeling experiences of others in response to them. This level of affect regulation will include the capacity to recognize and respond to the feelings of others with awareness and empathy. Thus, internalizing these early experiences of "feeling felt" becomes the basis for deepening a variety of later relationships with others: as a friend, colleague, lover, family member, and eventually partner and parent. Intersubjectively stated, the working model of one's own mind becomes the stepping-stone to developing a working model of the minds of others in reciprocal interaction with the self.

Self-reflection, whether focused on events, behaviors, past experiences, current feelings, or even thoughts, defines the ability to mentalize. Mentalization is a reflective mode, a mental state that permits one to view self and others as representations (Fonagy et al., 2002). Proceeding from a secure attachment base in infancy and early childhood, mentalization enables the individual to develop working models of self and others. When this function is impaired, nonreflective working models of self and others predominate and serve to distort current relationships, perpetuating an alien, disorganized self system. Because autonoesis, defined as the capacity for self-understanding of one's unique autobiography over time, requires reflection, and therefore, memory, the two terms are related. However, the term *autonoesis* differentiates the various neurobiological memory functions (implicit, explicit, event, etc.) as encodings in the frontal areas of the cerebral cortex. Mature functioning in the autonoetic mode permits "mental mind travel," backward in time as well as forward into the future, as experiences are attached to the self with a full array of contexts, affects, and perceptions (D. J. Siegel, 1999).

The developmental base for *secondary emotional experience* in adolescence, itself deriving from the affect regulation function, involves a complex hierarchy of competencies and is, consequently, never fully attained by anyone. Everyone struggles with the difficulty of recognizing and comprehending feelings, both their own and those of others. All individuals deploy defense mechanisms in a balancing act to manage, distort, or otherwise alter the impact on the psyche of potentially toxic feelings. Therefore significant elements of feeling states will frequently remain unconscious. Autonoesis, as well as knowing the minds of others, can be only partial.

Unconscious Metaphorical Thought

The Freudian view of the dynamic unconscious, the mechanism of repression proper (versus primal repression) and the elasticity of the repression barrier itself as it operates in the dream state (1900, 1905a, 1915b, 1915c), is not at all at odds with the cognitive processes of linguistic categorization that human minds employ to represent meaning through a rich matrix of conceptual metaphors. Nonconscious, awake-state metaphorical thought is automatic, not subject to conscious control, and effortless (Lackoff, 1997). Furthermore, this everyday, normal kind of thinking does not derive from the repression of traumatic conflicts in the classic drive defense paradigm (Burston, 1986). On the other hand, the various mechanisms in the dream state that operate to disguise or otherwise render ambiguous the deeper, latent meaning of the dream—displacement, exaggeration, representation by opposites (litotes) and by parts for wholes (metonymy), symbolization, reversal of affect, and condensation—are all remarkably similar to the ones involved in everyday, metaphorical renderings of experiences where irony, paradox, and figures of speech play a significant role (Lackoff, 1997). Also similar to the Freudian unconscious are the affects, culturally shared meanings, and inherent, narrated mythic systems that underlie each kind of thought, both manifest dream images and metaphor, at every level of awareness. For Lackoff and Freud, implicit in both systems is the notion that an unconscious but actively thinking mind, one that is simultaneously ongoing with consciousness, is a perfect way for not knowing what one actually knows without being aware of knowing it at one and the same time.

Dreaming represents a further rendering of symbolic meanings beyond the realm of the initial illusory world, the in-between world of creativity and constructed experience, where infant self-image and maternal object representations converge. The dream state is thus a subjective orbit of illusion within illusion, an additional symbolic world in which elements of the first illusionistic in-between space, involving infant and mother, meet other created and shared, intersubjective encounters with different objects, especially therapeutic ones. Through metaphorical thought, elements of the therapy dyad merge and re-emerge as day residues of the treatment relationship trigger dream images that partake of three core subjectivities: that of the therapist, that of the patient, and that inherent in the interrelationship between the two. This additional world of illusion, created as a result of the intersubjectivity of the patient and therapist, operates within what Ogden has termed the analytic third (1994).

While the first transitional object of early childhood must of necessity pass, or as Winnicott suggests, become psychologically absorbed, that is, "diffused . . . over the whole cultural field" of infant-mother relatedness (1951, p. 233), transitional processes themselves remain alive as fertile potentials for later constructions that are illusionistic and between self and object. With an "attention cathexis," when verbalized to another or retrospectively reviewed, these transitional renderings of subjective experiences are potentially adaptive, in that the primary process forms that metaphorical thoughts take, as dynamic, illusionistic, or between self and object, fuse semantic elements at the formal-operational, secondary-process level of mentation (Rose, 1980, 1996). Metaphorical dream images thereby serve to neutralize raw, energic drive elements of libido and aggression and simultaneously divorce them from the potential for immediate gratification and discharge. The consequent meanings of these metaphorical images, their mappings from the superordinate (myth and cultural belief principle) domain to the basic level domains of personal experience and the characteristics of the dreamer's personality traits and history, that is, his idiography (Lackoff, 1997), become the bridge to enhanced self-awareness and are integral to the mentalizing function within a consolidated identity. While similar to Ekstein's formulation of interpretation within the metaphor as a therapeutic activity that enables the adolescent to progress from "thoughtless action, to actionless thought, to thoughtful action" (1966), an intersubjectivist focus on metaphorical meanings emphasizes affects and the narration of experience, rather than the analysis of ego defenses (Levin, 1980).

Findings from neurobiological research have further informed, and confirmed, the multiple ways dreaming functions as the mind's vehicle for processing conflictual affects and dysphoric emotional states, particularly those involving fear, anger, guilt, shame, and anxiety. Neural networks can be altered later, as encoded and stored, implicit memory misalliances and ruptures in the holding environment are reworked in the dream state. Once retrieved and understood, these dream images may aid in the smoothing of a life narrative (D. J. Siegel, 1999; D. J. Siegel, 2007) as past and present, transference and reality become integrated into a more coherent identity. Empirical research, primarily the findings from imaging studies, suggests that brain activity during dreaming is both regionally, as well as biochemically, different than awake-state, conscious thought and non-REM sleep. The regions of the brain involved in REM sleep are the memory and affect centers: feedback loops from the cortical association areas reciprocally stimulate the thalamic, hippocampal-amygdalar complex (Krystal & Krystal, 1994).

In summary, metaphorical thought functions as a transitional form of activity between primary and secondary process thought. Thus, to the extent that advanced, secondary process elaboration of dream images leads to better adaptation to the environmental surround, metaphors operate as a royal road to conscious and purposeful reality testing. To the extent that metaphorical renderings within the dream open up new possibilities for creative solutions to conflicts, via reliance on magic and intuition in the domain of tacit knowledge (Polanyi, 1962, 1966), the primary process also matures as one becomes more imaginative and autoplastic in developing coping mechanisms (Hartmann, 1939; Rose, 1996). Boundaries, where they exist between the primary and secondary processes, become more fluid and permeable. Thus, metaphor, as a therapeutic tool, functions as a bridge from the unconscious to the preconscious-conscious system, from primary to secondary process thought, from global affect states to the differentiation of feelings, and from identity confusion to a new synthesis of self and object representations in the adolescent stage.

Case Illustrations

This intersubjective approach to the dynamic understanding of treatment processes differs significantly from the traditional point of view. One core assumption is that, because of its inherent phenomenology, it would be impossible to completely objectify the treatment relationship (Atwood & Stolorow, 1999). However, while ruling in subjectivity establishes a constructivist orientation, it does not necessarily follow that the requirement of objectivity is ruled out as a stance in understanding the clinical relationship. A related assumption is the way countertransference is understood, that is, more as a necessary condition for a successful treatment relationship than as an impediment to it. The constructivist point of view would be that the treatment relationship can be reality-tested through the lens of objectivity, as well as subjectively understood, experientially, as a clinical fact. Both points of view require meeting the various tests of validity, but each involves a different kind of proof. Thus, clinicians maintain an objective stance, but also factor in their own fluctuating, emotional reactions to clients as every bit as valid forms of clinical detail as a listing, for instance, of symptoms in the diagnostic statement. Monitoring the treatment relationship in this fashion, that is, attending to the various subjectivities of the dyad and including the intersubjectivity inherent in the relationship, means that therapy becomes more personal, meanings more mutually constructed, and enactments more context-dependent (Mischler, 1986).

This version of the therapeutic process departs significantly from the traditional view and involves an emerging paradigm shift from objectivity to subjective construction. Intersubjectivist research describes the processes of treatment, for example, transference and countertransference phenomena, establishing and maintaining the therapeutic alliance, working through and termination. Such clinical studies augment, but do not replace, outcome studies based on experimental, "evidence-based" procedures with statistical tests and measures at only two points in time, relatively static "events" involving a pre-test and a post-test (Leitenberg, 1973; Lucente, 1987). Solidarity becomes the goal of theory-building, as individuals are studied and understood in the context of their unique cultures and stories (Rorty, 1991). As therapists "dwell in" the treatment relationship, validity is established through thick description (Imre, 1982; Geertz, 1973). In the clinical relationship, however, therapeutic activity still involves all of the necessary, technical elements of exploration, explanation, confrontation, interpretation and universalization, and so on. Treatment does require, however, that therapists take the role more of an older uncle/aunt or special adult friend of the adolescent patient, rather than that of a distant authority figure (Meeks & Bernet, 2001; Murphy & Hirschberg, 1982), and self-disclose with greater facility (Basch, 1980; Palombo, 1987). As the patient's psychobiography gradually unfolds, the parts will be examined for the recurring themes and central concerns that pervade the client narrative. Dysfunctional repetitions and unfinished business from the genetic phases and past development are reworked in a constant dialectic involving the client's future potential and his past history, still alive in the present (Loewald, 1980a). Over time, treatment aims to understand these experiences as the narrative parts eventually give rise to the whole. All of this is constructed interpersonally. Just as there was no observed infant without an observing mother, there is no observed and observing patient without an observed and observing therapist.

Jeff presents as a more physically mature-looking teen than his fourteen years would suggest. He has been "passed along" academically by his teachers each year since the fifth grade because of his superior intelligence. Failing in each of his courses as the semester reaches its end because he obstinately refuses to do homework, Jeff spends a week cramming, on the brink of imminent failure, and earns a barely passing grade at the last minute. His boredom in the classroom is obvious. He daydreams incessantly and remains aloof from classroom interaction. He taxes the patience of his teachers, who recognize his immense potential. Because most are genuinely fond of him, they have typically attempted to involve Jeff's mother to help motivate him. However, after meeting with Jeff's obese, intrusively inappropriate and unempathic mother (she is an overbearing, 400-pound supervisor of nurses at a graded care facility for the elderly), they typically resign themselves to a lethargic acceptance of Jeff as a problem without a solution. Accompanied by his mother at the initial visit to my office, he is obviously uncomfortable in her presence and begins to withdraw, glassy-eyed, into an almost trance-like dissociative state, as she forcibly thrusts into my hand a copy of a psychological staff report dating back to the fifth grade that suggests a tentative diagnosis of attention deficit disorder. I agree to meet with each separately, but after the assessment and treatment recommendation has been formulated to share it with them together.

As Jeff settled comfortably into the initial phase of treatment, he fluently verbalized the major themes of his early adolescence as a frantic search for purpose, direction, and unity. He recollected that, on his fourteenth birthday, he became suddenly aware that he felt his life had been pointless and that time was against him. In response to my query about his fantasy life in the classroom, Jeff stated that he almost always daydreamed about being a soldier-warrior in search of justice, especially about capturing the leaders of al-Qaeda. His favorite childhood heroes were a blend of Rambo, Spider Man, the Caped Crusader, and the immortal warrior, Connor McLeod, the Highlander (from the movie with the same title), as well as countless images afforded by PlayStation and other software. I wondered about his nighttime dreams. He said many of them he remembered as continuations of his daytime reveries, as he drifted off to sleep, as well as the stimuli for his awake-state fantasies. His most notable dream always occurred in the last REM sequence before awakening.

Months later, as we further explored the psychosocial world of his personal heroes, he told me of his relationship with his favorite paternal uncle, an avid outdoorsman and landowner/farmer who resides in Saskatchewan. This decorated Marine Corps veteran of the Vietnam War always invites Jeff to visit him in the fall to hunt waterfowl as the "living sky" dramatically explodes with the wing beats of countless mallards, pintails, blue and green winged teal, widgeon and snow and Canada geese. Jeff subliminally recognizes that he has been chosen to represent the familial traditions of his Scottish forebears, a culture of previous generations of Saskatchewan farmers, both in reverence to nature and, at the same time, one with it, as the forests and vast fields of wheat and barley reflect a continual cycle of harvest and renewal, also in keeping with his heritage of mythic poet/warriors. In this session, I volunteer that I also have had a close relationship with a relative, two generations ahead of me, who became a consistent source of support during my childhood and adolescence, providing instruction in hunting and fishing, as well as modeling the concepts of fair chase, respect for the wonders of the natural environment, and a sense of connectedness with the land.

At an evening session, Jeff reported the following dream: I have become a commissioned officer and an Army Ranger. My unit has been sent to the Middle East and I have endured sandstorms, witnessed casualties as a result of ambush by partisan militia, and have barely escaped myself with minor injuries before confronting an al-Qaeda leader. I find myself alone, trapped in a cave facing the enemy. My assault rifle misfires and jams repeatedly, and I am in danger of being shot. A stranger dressed in civilian clothes is standing at my side as the rifle suddenly becomes a sixteenth-century broadsword that I use to capture the enemy.

After this session and on the same night, I (i.e., the therapist) had the following dream in the final REM sequence before awakening: I am walking down a totally colorless, foggy, and dimly lit urban street during twilight and see two deer in front of me running from something that I cannot see. Gradually, the black, white, and grey of the urban landscape turns into the African savannah, full of color, with only the street remaining as it is. The two deer are nowhere in sight, but I now see a lion behind me at one end of the street. I think to myself, "I am safe" and begin to run away but another lion, exactly like the first, suddenly appears in front of me; at the same time each lion begins to run towards me. I cannot find my rifle to defend myself, but reach into my pocket, locating my pistol, which I aim at the closest lion, just before it turns into a pen, prior to my awakening

The associations to my dream are, as in Jeff's dream: (1) I am both the hunter and the hunted, both prey and predator in an unfamiliar, wild country; (2) there is danger all around and the outcome of the encounter is uncertain; (3) weaponry either initially fails to function or cannot be located until the last minute. In addition, the deer/lions in my dream symbolize my patient, whose identity is also undergoing change. The dream mechanism of representation by opposites, litotes, is featured in my thought that "I am safe" when, in actuality, I am in dire jeopardy of imminent death. The key affect states in my dream include a mixture of fear at the prospect of being attacked, excitement as the dull grey urban scene transforms into the majestic beauty of the African savannah, and frustration. These are very similar to the affects my client experiences. Just as one of the lions is in my pistol sights at the very end of the dream, so my client becomes a better understood target of scrutiny, with my pen, in treatment. The day-residue elements of Jeff's dream which focused on his changing identity, and specifically my role as catalyst in the guise of the transference figure of the stranger/uncle, probably triggered my own dream about better understanding my role as his therapist and my own complementary countertransference interactions (Atwood et al., 1989) within the relationship dyad.

These mutually shared processes of timing, fitting together, and rhythmicity—an unconscious version of "I know, that you know, that I know"—have been described by Sander during the course of a half-century of his infant-mother research (1980, 2002). Such attunements are core to the experiences of "feeling felt." In a simultaneously poetic and empirically detailed vignette, a tired and fussy eight-day-old infant, cradled in her father's left arm, somehow signals the need for an empathic connection to safely fall asleep. The father responds with a split-second eye contact, returns to his interview with the research team, and without looking down extends his baby finger to the tiny clasp of his daughter—all without conscious awareness (Sander, 2002). Therapist and client share an intersubjectivity, as do deer and lions; however, each pair is unique and must construct the nature of their experience together. Elaborating on other shared elements of identity in the treatment dyad are themes of competition aggression, and mastery of conflict that are embedded in the metaphors of combat soldier and lion/hunter/prey. They clearly point to the active presence of an analytic third (Ogden, 1994) and a complementary, two-person shared unconscious system (Lyons-Ruth, 1999; Sander 2002).

Employed by the same company as her father, who is a senior vice president and a "lifer," nineteen-year-old Jennifer attends a community college as a part-time student following a brief, two-year career as a professional ballerina. After Jennifer suffered stress fractures in both ankles, one after another, which never fully healed, and to avoid future complications, her sports-specialist orthopedist recommended a different occupation, citing grim statistics of likely, early-onset arthritis and chronic pain. Because she was full-figured, large-boned, and tall, Jennifer's physique had always been an impediment to attaining the grace and agility required of a ballerina. As an adolescent, she had strenuously sought to control her weight with dieting and constant exercise. When these measures failed, she resorted to purging regimens symptomatic of bulimia. Consequently, lack of proper nutrition and calcium deficiency played a significant role in her fractures.

Living alone in an apartment near campus, she was isolated and friendless. Companionship consisted of frequent, intrusive visits by her parents who would stock her refrigerator with ample supplies of the three food groups and continually admonish her to eat three square meals daily. My initial strategy with Jennifer was to invite her to tell me about her life in ballet from age six and about her family life from childhood through adolescence. She described her discomfort with her body, the teasing to which others in her various ballet troupes had subjected her, and the unrelenting battles with her parents around mealtime. However, she also described her identification with her father, stating proudly that he was as "strong as a bull" and nearly as large, a virtual opposite to the lithe figure of her petite mother. I noted my own preoccupation as an adolescent with athletics, in my case, competitive swimming, with its peer competition, endless practices, early burnout, and the weight and strength concerns permeating the sport. I joked that the only difference between our experiences had to do with my keeping weight on and her taking weight off.

After this self-disclosure, Jennifer reported, in our next session, having the following dream that very night: a small, graceful child receives a beautiful bouquet of roses after some kind of performance with an audience looking on and applauding her. As the stage becomes more familiar, I recognize it as the dance center where I danced the lead roles in ballet performances when I was in high school. The child quickly becomes an adult, large-boned and clumsy and just as I think to myself "this must be me," the ballerina turns into a rhinoceros still dressed in a pink tutu. She tries to dance, and is surprisingly light on her feet, but the audience has stopped applauding and I sense disapproval. That very night I had a dream, similar in detail to the manifest content I reported earlier immediately after Jeff's dream.

Jennifer's dream reflects her identity confusion through metaphorical statement about her body image. Representation by opposites (litotes) is abundant. The applauding audience suggests a public forum where the exact opposite, the psychic reality of a private and personal secret, is about to be revealed. The sheer bulk of the rhinoceros masks the opposing wish to be petite. At the manifest level, the imagery denotes a beautiful child, a star, who grows up to be a rhinoceros (a *ballerhino*) that is, paradoxically, light on its feet, graceful, and coordinated. Large, immensely strong, and potentially combative, the rhinoceros also conveys Jennifer's unspoken anger at the early loss of her chosen career and her frustration with the negative audience, the parents whom she tried endlessly to win over, and would now like to charge, but whom she has introjected as bad object representations. Implied also is the change from their initial approval of her as a small child and her ambivalently internalized image as a good self.

In her dream, Jennifer relives her life through two dominant and interconnected metaphoric images: a ballerina and an angry rhinoceros. Concretely, the ponderous rhinoceros in the dream further signifies her concern with her weight as an impediment to her career as a ballerina; at a deeper level, it alludes to the "heavy weight" of the burdens she carries with her daily. The target domain of being a successful ballerina is mapped onto the source domain of large, aggressive beasts (Lackoff, 1987, 1997). Significantly, it is the lower life form (from the point of view of the great chain of being, with humankind at the peak) that now dominates the dream. Implied is Jennifer's fall from an earlier grace. The conceptual metaphor has hidden elements as well. First is an identification with her father whose body build and raw physical strength and stamina she also possesses. This identification carries with it a linkage to her familial, remote, and mythic past. Her parents' cultural ancestry was eastern European. Working the land in a harsh, rural environment required the fortitude and endurance of the "country Polish" who persevered century after century. Secondly, as an endangered species, rhinoceroses are special and deserve understanding, care, and protection. Finally, being large and very graceful are not at all mutually exclusive.

In my dream, beast imagery, as it does in Jennifer's, expresses an identification with the qualities of two species: deer and lions. Lions possess strength as they are the kings of the beasts. My astrological sign is Leo the Lion, whose attributes include generosity, trustworthiness, and loyalty. One of my favorite childhood heroes from history was King Richard the Lion-hearted who returned from the Crusades to rescue England from a tyrant. That two deer change into lions, and that a child grows up to briefly become an adult, who quickly transforms into a rhinoceros, link themes of shared elements of identity from one dreamer to another. In the context of therapy, as in everyday life, "one person's dream can have a powerful meaning for others" (Lackoff, 1997, p. 108) at all levels of awareness.

A vast literature exists on the subjects of adolescent identity formation and identity confusion. This literature, from traditional developmental theory, suggests that the following are necessary for closure as a stable adolescent identity: mature, psychosexual drive organization, that is, genitality, and a sexuality that expresses itself via arousal for a preferred, erotic object (S. Freud, 1905b, 1923,

1924; Erikson, 1959); autonomous independent functioning and separation from childhood love objects (a second individuation process) with capacities for object and self constancy (Masterson, 1972; Kernberg, 1966; Mahler et al., 1975; Blos, 1967); moral reasoning utilizing hypothetico-deductive thought and internalized ego ideals (Kohlberg, 1976; Gilligan, 1982; Piaget, 1950; Blos, 1962); an adulto-morphic body image, rooted in one's core gender as unambiguously male or female (Stoller, 1968); and an evolved, superordinate ego-superego system that organizes the various components of the personality (Blanck & Blanck, 1974, 1986). All of these theoretical formulations seem to imply that the various elements (structures, capacities, and internalizations), once attained, remain as fixed and unchanging after the adolescent's passage through Erikson's stage of identity versus identity diffusion (1963).

Winnicott proposed a different way to conceptualize identity, locating the core of identity in the experiences of the true self (1950, 1958, 1960a). Two of the most notable features of this structure are its privacy and the sense of an ongoing, uninterrupted continuity of being, over time, within a personal body schema. In the adolescent stage, as the true self becomes more integrated through self-narration, mentalization, and autonoesis, core elements of identity begin to consolidate as long-term, autobiographical representations of experience become permanently stored in explicit memory. Bypassing the hippocampus, these elements of core identity, involving "the sense of recollection . . . from the past," merely require an effortless act of attention to be retrieved (D. J. Siegel, 1999, p. 65). For both Jennifer and Jeff, dreaming and their narrations as subjective episodes aided the process of their "cortical consolidation" of representations from their past histories into the present.

Freud proposed that, at birth, the "system unconscious" contained multiple inheritances from previous generations of ancestors, including the potential influences of their unique, mythic, and cultural endowments (S. Freud, 1915c). In classic drive theory terms, the linkage of current recollections involving episodes of remembered experience, when juxtaposed to the unconscious, mythic elements (the drive-determined, latent, and metaphorical dream images) of Jeff's and Jennifer's ancestral endowments, permitted a new reorganization of previously unintegrated self and object representations. This new functional identity whole included the associated vitality affects that are diffused throughout the personality. While Jeff's final dream image signified himself as an Army Ranger,

it was his Scottish broadsword—symbolizing his mythic heritage as a warrior—
that facilitated the capture of the enemy. The adaptive, false self appears in the
guise of the uniform, the outer covering that protects the true self represented
by the broadsword.

The elements of the true self, reflected in all three dreams, are inherent in
the imagery of the beasts and warriors, mythic pasts, and the feeling states and
vitality affects relative to the drives. Each dream also attests to the presence of
elements of the false self, that is, the public, social side of identity that is constructed through interactions with the environment of others. These "me selves"
(Erikson, 1968) together make up the structure of the false self and are functional to the extent that they protect the privacy of the true self from invasion.
It is the task of the adaptive, false self to permit expression of the true self, without excessive interference or control from the demands of the outer environment. At the same time, there exists no clear line of demarcation separating the
true from the false self; rather, the former continually infuses the adaptive false
self with rich personal meanings. Finally, these two selves, the true and the false,
are not binary construction; they blend into one another and therefore share a
permeable membrane that permits each self to influence the other.

In a later paper that continued many references to the adolescent passage
and identity formation, Winnicott expanded his formulation to include a third
area of self-structure between the true self and the false self (1963). While retaining the privacy of the true self (the core that remains forever unknown to others
and immune to the reality principle), he described an intermediate area that was
both pleasurable and explicitly communicated. This intermediate area serves as
an adaptive compromise with the demands of culture (role performance and
conformity) in the multiple contexts of public life. Simultaneously congruent
with the inner needs of the individual and the outer demands of the environment, this intermediate area of identity, in healthy functioning, neither distorts,
inhibits, contradicts, nor replaces the expression of the true self. In all three
dreams, the latent content of the metaphorical images at their deepest level, to
the extent that they attest to the presence of the true selves, will probably remain, forever, as mysteries to others; thus, each image refers to, alludes to, and
signifies a true-self meaning, but does not perfectly equate with the true self of
the dreamer, which remains permanently closed off from open communication
with the outside world.

Jeff's daytime and nightly preoccupation with weaponry, combat, victory over evil forces, and the strength of warriors gradually permitted a more adaptive false self, in the intermediate range of identity, to emerge in the context of his classroom activities and choice of a potential occupation. Always an avid reader of current culture, best-selling action novels (but never of homework assignments!), his attention now turned to the biographies of famous firearm inventors—three men of genius from Germany, the United States, and Russia. For his English class, he chose to report on the lives of John Browning, Mikhail Kalashnikov, and Georg Luger, the inspirational designers of the autoloading and fully automatic pistols and rifles that were involved in the military transformations of the world over the course of the twentieth century. He also began to speculate on a career path that would lead from his academic interest in military science to a college degree from one of the military institutes and a commission as an officer on graduation. Noting that a military officer must also be able to communicate with, as well as lead troops, and following his natural talent for extemporaneous speaking, he joined the high school debate team to further enhance his verbal and interpersonal skills in "polite" combat. These various activities surrounding the use of words—reading, writing, and speaking—promoted his greater facility in the regulation of his affects and furthered his individuation.

It is the sense of effectance (White, 1959, 1963) that promotes the individual's gradual independence from external objects. This sense of effectance, as a motivational force with drive status equal to libido and aggression, also assists in the further consolidating of identity, as the adolescent increasingly displays a sense of personal self-agency, a maturing of the capacity to make choices that are self-willed rather than other-controlled (D. N. Stern, 1985; Fonagy et al., 2002). The adolescent further differentiates and individuates, a second time, from the internalized object representations of the parents of childhood. Remaining in her sadness and self-reflecting at the same time, Jennifer was able to make choices that included adaptations to the painful reality of her physical limitations, as well as relying on a multitude of other talents that she had defensively marginalized as unimportant. In addition to ballet, she had also expressed herself in the performing arts in high school plays and had been an avid member of choruses throughout her latency years. Her "mental time travel" back to these childhood and early adolescence experiences, involving mastery in these psychosocial dimensions, increased her autonoesis and self-acceptance. She auditioned for, and won, lead roles in semi-professional and community-based, choreographed productions of famous Broadway musicals. Her adaptive false self, in the intermediate range of her identity, began to flourish, manifesting itself in her singing, dancing, and acting. These environmental activities were multi-determined. While providing peer support and reducing her tendency to withdraw, they also affirmed the true self, that is, her raw, physical presence and the vitality affects associated with the pleasurable feelings of a graceful body in motion and in being a songstress. In this fashion the "me self" system of actress, dancer, and singer facilitated the consolidating of an identity that was simultaneously adaptive to the social environment but also true to her core self.

My professional roles, intellectual life, and mission all lie in the intermediate range of identity, between the true and the adaptive false self. The brilliant explosion of color, as the urban grey of the city becomes the African savannah, expresses the vibrancy and vitality of the true self in interaction with mighty carnivores: lion and clinician are one and the same. Yet, the presence of the deer, two herbivores, and denizens of the urban environment where I practice, suggest the ongoing presence of an adaptive false self, a quieter and more peaceful version of the beast within. The pen symbolizes that, at times, it can be mightier than the sword in my attempts to orchestrate the therapies and to better understand and communicate with Jeff and Jennifer. Like the pistol, the pen is an instrument, the latter being merely a more refined version of the former that "aims" at a deeper understanding, through insight, after proper "sighting in" on the targets of scrutiny.

If there exist as many worlds as there are people (Mischler, 1986; Bruner, 1986; Rorty, 1991) and, if there are as many intermediate realms of illusion within illusion as there are dreamers, then the central concern of adolescence is to construct one's place in one's own world and one's place in the world of significant others. At the same time, a second individuation is occurring that propels the adolescent forward into the environment and prepares him or her for adult responsibilities, thus providing some measure of closure on the latency years and childhood dependencies. Mahler's phrasing of the goal of the separation experience, "on the way to object constancy," implies a journey, a work-in-progress that will forever remain unfinished. So it would also seem to be as the adolescent embarks on a long journey through adulthood "on the way to consolidating identity." In the domain of emotion, recognizing feelings in self and others and developing fuller control over the expression of complex affect states will also remain a task that can never be fully mastered. In all of these regards, relative to identity, affect regulation, autonoesis, and mentalizing self and others, presenting these three dreams permitted a joining of cognitive/linguistic psychology and psychodynamic theory with a focus on the ideas of Winnicott, Freud, Lackoff, and the intersubjectivists. The process demonstrated the ease with which the Freudian unconscious, especially surrounding the dreamers' uses of hyperbole, litotes, symbolization, displacement, and metonymy, fit together with the latent and manifest imagery afforded by metaphorical thought at all levels of awareness.

Qualitative Clinical Inquiry

As in all treatment research where the goal is knowledge development and its refinement, the assessment of the research report—the results, findings, and the conclusions, whether derived from quantitative or qualitative methodologies—must meet basic guidelines for ensuring their validity, relevance, accuracy, and credibility. In his classic critique of the case narrative report as a leap from the privacy of the clinical office setting into the public domain and citing Freud's case of Dora (1905a), Spence argued for a "new genre" of case analyses in which the reader is invited to be the judge of the adequacy of the clinical evidence to substantiate the author's conclusion, rather than the latter's interpretations of cause and effect, dazzling conclusions, and rhetorical skills as an omniscient storyteller (1986). When the clinical narrative conforms to the basic principles for assessing validity and relevance, the intensive case study as a special form of qualitative clinical inquiry meets the conditions for knowledge building and theory development. It is not that good writing is necessarily suspect; however, it is not a sufficient basis for explanation nor does it replace the factual account.

In the intensive case study approach the clinical knowledge bank that is expanded and the developmental theory that is verified through a detailed explication of a clinical narrative must meet specific criteria for establishing a quality research product according to the following five dimensions of assessment (Mays & Pope, 1996). First is the consistency of the theoretical concepts as they correspond to the data collected. This dimension of assessment is the extent to which construct validity has been demonstrated and also bears upon the reliability of the data collection procedures. A second dimension of assessment is the thoroughness and detail with which the report describes both the culture and the context of the treatment, including the relevant therapist and client psychosocial surrounds. Third is the adequacy of the sampling plan, that is, patient selection and goodness of fit as these relate to the focus of study. The fourth dimension involves the clarity of the research question and the extent to which it is infused throughout the report. Finally there is the reflexivity of the account itself, how the researcher demonstrates self-reflection on the impact of the research methods, that is, his use of self on the clinical data obtained and his client's responses in the treatment relationship. To the extent that the research report and the clinical narrative answer concerns in these critical areas, qualitative inquiry through the microanalysis of a psychotherapeutic process becomes a valid vehicle for theory building. The external validity of the case study, the potential for the clinical research to generalize to other settings and other client/therapist dyads, hinges on the coherence of the narrative report and on the data collection and analysis procedures being sufficiently systematic to produce an "audit trail," a prescription or formula for other clinicians to follow for replication in other settings with similar clients. Quantitative studies with designs utilizing empirical methods, inferential statistics, and the controls that are modeled on the pristine laboratory experiment simply cannot ask the most intriguing research questions in the clinical realm, the ones that inhere in the intersubjective matrix of client self, therapist self, and their shared relational orbit in between.

Historically, the early pursuit of clinically relevant knowledge in social work began with the intensive case study of psychosocially significant person-in-situation variables (Richmond, 1917; Zimbalist, 1977). Within virtually all of the helping professions and beginning in the 1950s, however, this traditional form of clinical knowledge development was supplanted by rigorous group research designs that utilized elaborate controls and a statistical basis for inference (random sampling techniques and probability statements), ostensibly to reassure the consumer that chance factors alone might explain treatment outcomes only a very few times in a hundred or so similar trials. It is now widely accepted that the positivist conception of the scientific method is both limited and frequently misdirected as a research underpinning in the social and psychological sciences and for the helping professions in general. Research methods based on the positivist tradition assume that the rules of experimental design—the manipulation and control of variables, random sampling and random assignment, the aseptic setting of the laboratory, the pursuit of general laws of behavior that apply universally to everyone irrespective of context and culture, and the purity of mathematical calculations that formalize the research findings—apply equally to the study of human development, social relationships, and psychotherapy (Mischler, 1986). However, the same positivist model and its epistemological base that proved successful in the building of the natural sciences, for example, biology and physics, has only limited utility in clinical research.

The tensions within social work, and within most of the helping and counseling professions in general, that underlie much of this controversy over clinical practice and its relationship to research and knowledge building—qualitative versus quantitative measurements; constructivism versus positivism; subjectivity and bias versus objectivity, neutrality, and restraint; the ecological perspective versus empiricism; the proper place of fact, feeling, and belief; and explanation as a more reasoned approach to the use of theory than prediction of outcome—have been reviewed elsewhere, as have their philosophical assumptive bases (Wodarski & Bagarozzi, 1979; Saleebey, 1979; Heineman, 1981; Heineman-Pieper, 1985; Mullen, 1985). The tensions, however, continue unabated.

Moreover, in one of the most influential monographs to guide the epistemology of research-oriented social workers, particularly those who take an adamant empiricist stance to knowledge building within the profession, the authors state unequivocally that the case study possesses "almost no scientific value" as a method of establishing a relationship between variables in a research hypothesis, that is, between an antecedent condition and a later outcome occurrence (Campbell & Stanley, 1963, p. 6; Cook & Campbell, 1979). This positivist assertion cannot be accepted at face value. Rather, the question would be how and where the case study can best serve the scientific goals of discovery, classification of concepts, construct validation, and knowledge refinement.

Partly due to numerous outcries from practicing professionals that group designs tended only to scratch the surface of treatment-related concerns in the therapist and client domains, and that more and more design rigor was being applied to learn significantly less and less about treatment and clients, the single organism approach was once heralded as an answer to the dilemma of how to remain scientific in approach, yet client-centered at the same time (Reid, 1972; Howe, 1974; Jayaratne, 1977; Reid & Epstein, 1977). While useful for charting client change (B) in explicit, baseline target behaviors (A) resulting from highly specific techniques—programmed therapist activities versus the inert psychotherapeutic features inherent within the clinician (Strupp, 1973)—single subject methodologies have not, in the main, proven equal to their original promise. While a full critique of the reasons for this lack is not the purpose of this chapter, two glaring flaws of single organism study are central to themes that will be developed later.

First, in the ethical realm of the professional ego ideal, it is unconscionable to expose a client to an ameliorating intervention (B) and later withdraw it, hoping for a return to baseline (A) merely to demonstrate the saliency of a cause-effect inference. Second, it is categorically unsound in the realm of logical mentation to suggest the symmetry of machine and man. That is, it may be feasible to measure a car's improved acceleration and economy when fuel injection has replaced at the intake manifold the inefficient two-barrel carburetor because the car itself remains constant before, during, and after the manipulations. However, it is not so with human subjects. Clients are affected, and deeply, as a result of therapeutic activity. Withdrawing practice interventions does not reinstate clients to their original condition, and it is unrealistic to think that one can manipulate a client system without acknowledging responsibility for effects and changes in the treatment process. For better and for worse, technical activity is cumulative, additive, and transforming.

In light of the above considerations, it would seem that some compromises would be in order between the laboratory precision of the classic, nomothetic before–after true experiment, the single organism ideographic approach, and the traditional intensive case study. This chapter will address the complementarity of these methodologies (Jayaratne, 1977) and offers a relativist position rather than asserting that qualitative and quantitative research designs are discrete and unconnected. No suggestion is made that a preference hierarchy should exist for the inherent scientific superiority of one research methodology over another. The upshot of this analysis would be to facilitate a consideration of qualitative methodology as a guide to clinical inquiry and to elevate the classic case study to its rightful position, mindful of certain parameters, as a research method par excellence unto itself. Such an integrative approach recognizes the intrinsic mutuality of practice, the pursuit of clinical knowledge, and the advancement of theory.

Most professionals, social workers and practitioners with graduate degrees in the related counseling disciplines, particularly those who will seek clinical positions as career paths, differ predictably from their counterparts in clinical psychology, counseling psychology, and education (Kirk & Kolevzon, 1978) who will remain in academic settings. Their particular abilities ally more easily with a non-statistical, non-laboratory approach to the dilemmas of the human condition (Linn & Greenwald, 1974) where affective life and the realm of emotion remain fundamental. The intensive case study of a single individual (or family) over time is ideally suited to the humane examination of the whole person in his particular, unique environment rather than as an abbreviated cross-section. For practicing professionals the case study approach is unassailably empathy-promoting and individualizing. The former is achieved when the therapist is validated in his identification with the client's discomfort, disability, or dysfunction. It is individualizing because the clinician ultimately is encouraged to develop the capacity to differentiate his own experiencing from that of his client and his client's experiences from those of other clients.

The intensive case study's particular strength, the examination in minute detail of the salient clinical features of the client's history and life course narrative, is also the source of its tie to one of the fundamental principles underlying the implementation of any clinical research endeavor. This is that every independent variable, no matter how narrowly operationalized, is actually multivariate in its ultimate impact, and that every dependent variable can be understood best as likewise multivariate in its component outcome structure. Therefore, disentangling these antecedent, interactive, intervening, and coexisting processes from one another in the research enterprise is the necessary correlate to the practitioner performing the same tasks, later, in the privacy of the clinical or agency setting. The case study, utilized as a heuristic learning tool in the above fashion, helps clinicians develop rival hypotheses that provide alternative conceptualizations for developmental outcomes and alternative explanations for the effects of treatment. This enhances a beginning appreciation for environments that are ameliorating, average, and expectable, and, as well, for ones that are only marginally so. Clinician cognitions over time tend to move from the concrete to reveal a more formal operational, hypothetico-deductive sophistication which will pave the way for the future refinement of their clinical skills. Finally, the case study's presentation of inherently complex detail, and its rootedness in multicausal processes, eschews simple one-way univariate cause explanations for simple one-way univariate effects (Kerlinger, 1973). It thus serves each and every time, and refreshingly so, to refute simplistic reductionistic propositions that enjoy no realistic place in complex clinical practice or in treatment outcome and clinical process research.

From the above, it is obvious that the case study can be a tremendous aid in conceptualizing the complexity of the relationships between variables in a clinical research hypothesis. Such relationship complexities inhere in most psychodynamically oriented studies that highlight elements of client assessment, personality development, and choice of intervention. An illustrative example, and one by all means representative of the bountiful selection available to clinical researchers, is the report of "A case of paranoia running counter to the psychoanalytical theory of the disease" (S. Freud, 1915a). In this early study, the author described the clinically relevant history of an attractive young woman who had recently contacted a lawyer to prepare a suit against her former male lover. Her complaint (in retrospect determined to be a delusion) consisted of the unshakable belief that her lover and colleague, in collusion with her older female supervisor at work, had conspired to expose her to public humiliation with scandalizing photographs taken of her, unaware, in flagrante delicto, in the act of lovemaking. Freud predicated her persecutory delusions on (1) an internal personality change versus an external cause, the lover and supervisor being the feared but now despised objects of her projective defenses as well as the transparent and symbolic original love objects of the oedipal phase occasioned by a return of the repressed; and (2) the fact that the camera at the turn of the century resembled the modern-day refrigerator more than an Instamatic, was not conducive to easy concealment in tiny bachelor parlors, and tended to make atrociously loud noises when operated, as well as announcing its presence with such other obvious signs as billowing clouds of smoke. If one, therefore, concurs with Freud that a delusional process—paranoid persecutory symptoms—had emerged rather than a real attack involving conspirators, a hidden camera, and its operator on an otherwise emotionally stable but wronged, reality-oriented, and libidinally object-constant young woman, the variables can be conceptualized and ordered with precision and clarity.

First, the independent variable can be understood as the stimulus event, in short as the newfound love relationship with the boyfriend. Unraveling the action of the independent variable and its main effects on the antecedent, stable person-in-situation configuration of the client would involve noting the following developments: a return of the repressed oedipal history with its positive and negative arrest constellations; the unconscious and incestuous equation of love for a man (a non-family member) with oedipal-phase love for her father at the age of four; and the regressive solution of renouncing her object libidinal heterosexual position for the safer anaclitic attachment to a disguised maternal figure (and the narcissistically overdetermined parental imago).

Second, the dependent and, third, the intervening variables of this study lend themselves to similar analyses in this richly textured case summary. Dependent variables usually are understood as manifestations of change, or as effects revealed by measurements of outcome over time, proceeding from the stimulus. In this instance, the love affair produced particularly strong reactions in this young woman. They can be understood as her symptoms, her delusional beliefs and attendant anxieties, suspicious attitude, ambivalent affects, and reproachful behaviors (the threat of litigation) toward her lover. Because a relatively stable preexisting baseline state of apparent (pseudo-) adaptation had existed prior to the affair, the above analysis readily accords with the time sequence of "before-after" necessary to establish an initial basis for the inferring of covariation.

However, it must be pointed out that powerful intervening influences also compete for some of the variance typifying the young woman's reaction. This intervening multivariate network that might reasonably qualify the action of the independent variable consisted of the patient's unique constitutional sensitivities (perhaps she had always possessed an internal ego weakness predisposing her to interpersonal misperceptions and errors of judgment bipersonally); heredity (this was but a manic phase of a cyclical bipolar affective disorder surfacing for the first time in early adulthood but predicted by the chromosomes carried through preceding generations); her current home environment (maybe her roommate had been cruelly jilted by a recent boyfriend and this overreaction represented but a temporary, short-lived hyper-identification through altruistic surrender); and a host of other factors, for example, the Victorian moral climate (culture), macrohistory and economics, and the biases, representing error variance, that could accompany the tallies of unreliable measurements and invalid inferences drawn by the author and the referral source (the lawyer). Finally, further confounding the situation are significant interaction effects, for it must be remembered that the young litigant brought with her, to the attorney and his consultant, a host of organismic variables. She thus self-selected, as it were, into the affair because either she chose the relationship herself or consented to be the one chosen.

In summary, then, case studies typically afford practitioners richly textured client histories that promote their professional development in areas involving both skill sets and knowledge. First, rather than a sparse, slice-of-life, brief symptom cluster checklist of problem behaviors, case studies provide sufficient detail to make differential diagnosis mandatory rather than a sterile, pro forma textbook exercise. Second, over time, professionals can be observed to progress gradually from gross sympathetic reactions to clients (defensive overidentifications) to empathy-building awareness based on self-understanding and introspection. Third, because all case study reviews are retrospective and ex post facto, the significance of multicausality and systems thinking, appreciation for the fallacy of *post hoc ergo propter hoc* (Kerlinger, 1973), and a non-reductionistic practitioner frame of reference are repeatedly highlighted each and every time a single case is studied in detail. And finally, there is no shortage of exemplary case studies, classics in the literature that are tailor-made for the advanced learning of clinical process and clinical research applications. From a large and varied population the following is but a purposive, nonexhaustive sampling of these classics: S. Freud, 1905a, 1909a, 1911b; Blos, 1970; Goldberg, 1978; Goldstein & Palmer, 1978; Giovacchini, 1979; Basch, 1980; Fraiberg, 1981; Murphy & Hirschberg, 1982; Boyer, 1983; Strean, 1984; Zentner, 1984.

Sampling

At the outset, it must be acknowledged that case study research is vulnerable, as are all exploratory-formulative designs, to a number of criticisms. Without probability sampling as the basis for case selection, generalizing a study's conclusions to a larger group must be undertaken with considerable caution (this is a threat to external validity; Campbell & Stanley, 1963). Lacking controls that permit meaningful comparisons between cases at early and later points in time, the internal validity of measurements is also jeopardized. When a random assignment procedure to at least two initially equal conditions has not been employed, the measurements of the effects of an independent variable's manipulation (its presence and absence) cannot be reliably or validly assessed due to powerful competing explanations for the study's outcome. These rival hypotheses, ones based on such intervening and uncontrollable variables as history, selection, regression to the mean, maturation/development, instrument decay, and testing effects, represent different versions of the same story, calling into question which is the original and which is counterfeit. These limitations, once placed in their proper perspective, that is, within the context of the evolution of clinical theory, pale in comparison to the case study's manifest virtues as a vehicle for research into clinical processes. In the remainder of this chapter, the following strengths of the intensive single case study will be addressed: sampling, internal validity, and construct validation.

The problem of knowing to whom to generalize a study's findings is ubiquitous and universal across the wide spectrum of research designs. Philosophically, induction can never be fully justified because logically one can only guess at processes but partially understood. Even when there has been a flawless sample selection process with matching prior to random assignment, as in the usual social psychology laboratory experiment, certainty of extrapolation from sample to population is impossible. Laboratory subjects are inherently different from non-laboratory subjects; likewise, adolescents who seek treatment differ markedly from those adolescents who are similarly troubled but do not seek treatment. When the population has been sufficiently identified of all eighteen-year-old Caucasian males, indigenous to the Midwest, conservative in their outlook, and middle class in their strivings and affiliations, who likewise share a debilitating spider phobia that propels them into therapy, such a group will diverge significantly from their suffering twins who do not seek help. The most dramatic sampling errors of all apply to populations clinical researchers do not study directly but about whom they draw uncritical and erroneous inferences of similarity of characteristics, for example, the assumption of a universal debility-loss model to describe the aging process (Gutmann, 1980). To show that findings from one study apply elsewhere equally, researchers will always have to replicate with other samples.

Single case methodology cautiously rejects, as unrealistic, sweeping pronouncements that research findings are uniformly generalizable to any larger population. This criticism, of course, the lack of a sampling strategy, has always been considered the most troublesome in evaluating the usefulness of idiographic single organism research. However, in the intensive case study approach a modification of sampling strategy, preserving the principle but altering the technique, enables the researcher-clinician to closely approximate his target population. A mathematically calculated confidence interval has nothing to do with this procedure. Instead, by specifying the clinical population one desires to treat, and by maximizing the likelihood that the client chosen fully resembles the characteristics of the group to which he will later generalize the study's results, the researcher satisfies the purpose underlying any careful random selection process which is the equation of the homogeneity of sample and population.

Rather than selecting, at random, from the entire population its elements in all of their diversity, range, and variation, this strategy locates, on the basis of all the clinical and theoretical knowledge available, a client who fits the model. This procedure, conceptually, bears a similarity to that employed by biomedical researchers who experimentally determine the statistical probability of tumor outcomes from alleged carcinogens using animal populations in which lineages, hence genetics, have been fully controlled.

Because each discrete, hard-won scintilla of clinical knowledge really amounts to merely a "selectively retained tentative" (Campbell & Stanley, 1963, p. 4), the successfully planned case study will utilize all available knowledge, prior to the selection of the case, bearing on demographics, diagnostics, and development. The literature review would be its most critical dimension, and the implications of treatment would bear on the rigor of the sampling strategy. The task would then become, once a representative case had been chosen, to distinguish the findings in the light of this current prior clinical knowledge of the universe.

An illustration is in order for such a procedure. For thirty years, the border-line syndrome has been the subject of clinical inquiry. At this juncture, there would appear to exist a sufficient body of knowledge to describe the population of clients who present with this disorder, displaying recognizable background developmental histories in the attachment phases and in the second separation-individuation stage of adolescence, characteristic current levels of ego function-ing, and interpersonal behaviors likely to sustain such diagnoses from a cadre of experienced observer-clinicians. The model for assessing such a borderline popu-lation on a large scale would locate the individual's object relations arrest in the separation-individuation substages of development (Masterson, 1972; Blanck & Blanck, 1974; Mahler et al., 1975; Edwards, 1976). The drive-defense constellation and other ego functioning influences have been fully described as well (Knight, 1953; Kernberg, 1967; Gunderson & Singer, 1975; Palombo & Feigon, 1984). Finally, tolerances for intimacy, understanding of others, and mutuality of libidi-nal gratifications are constructs that could be used to profile a borderline client's interpersonal pursuits that should be clinically recognizable. Lacking object and self-constancy, such a client would present with identity confusion and tend to fragment, find it difficult to comfort self in times of emotional crisis, be more likely to exploit others for simple need gratification, lack the capacity to choose wisely a partner capable of giving understanding and object libidinal caring, and be unable to sustain a self-observing position in close relationships. Exacerbation of the intrapsychic conflicts and interpersonal tensions experienced by such a client when environmental stressors such as poverty, discrimination, and institu-tional exploitation occur would contribute to a more complete clinical picture of the person-in-situation configuration and enhance the generalizability of the case to populations that large numbers of social workers typically serve. The selection from this population of a single case, predicated on the above model, would satisfy the requirements for cautiously generalizing the outcome of treatment to a larger group of borderline clients. It in no way detracts from an appreciation for, and full recognition of, each and every client's individual differences.

Internal Validity

As the in-depth study of psychodynamic treatment has gradually freed itself from the shackles of behaviorism and the positivist/empiricist goals of objectifying and locating knowledge as separate, apart from, and outside of the experiencing person who knows it, the philosophical perspective guiding this paradigm shift has become increasingly post-positivist, intersubjective, and constructivist in all of its essential underpinnings. This pursuit of clinical knowledge, conceptualizing its processes in new and enlightening ways, is a research of discovery that rejects the mind/body and cognition/emotion dualisms that have always pervaded experimental models. Instead of ruling out the myriad effects on the client system of such variables as culture, diversity, context, myth and ritual, affect, and nonconscious mentation, intensive case analysis actively directs its focus to understand these as researchable elements of experience within the person, as clinician/researchers come to know their clients more completely, more deeply, more incisively, and with greater clarity.

A richly endowed fund of clinical understanding consists of subsidiary knowledge of the client within the clinician's tacit domain of relational knowing (Polanyi, 1962, 1966; Polanyi & Prosch, 1975) and provides the foundation for informed communication at all levels of awareness. This knowledge in the tacit dimension includes the clinician's own self-representations of experience as they correlate with the life narratives of his clients. As he immerses himself, imaginatively, in these ever-fluctuating identifications, his intuitive impressions promote further self-reflection and prompt insights that enable him to retrace the life course of his client. Clinical intuition in the tacit dimension derives from "dwelling in" (Polanyi & Prosch, 1975, p. 61) the client's present and in his past history to come to a more comprehensive, dynamic understanding, that is, a working model of the mind of the client. This "dwelling in" amounts to a focused concentration on the clinical material in all of its nonverbal and affective dimensions. Its aim is to discover the hidden clues that have hindered the client's search for coherence and integration.

The detailed case studies of adolescent clients in the preceding chapters operationalized a therapeutic approach to the treatment relationship that can be conceptualized as intersubjective, mentalizing, and psychodynamically informed. In each of the psychotherapies the observations—that is, the clinical data that emerged as phenomena for study, reflection, analysis, and written discourse—were twofold, consisting, first, of moment-by-moment, minute products of interpersonal and intrapsychic interview process and second, of overall indicators of client change, that is, treatment outcomes, from the initial assessment to termination. None of these measurements, whether of process or outcome, utilized standardized research instruments or schedules; instead, the clinical data collection instrument was the therapist who was variously the subject as well as the object of study, the observer as well as the observed, and as much a focus of clinical inquiry as the client.

The ability to maintain an "evenly suspended attention" (S. Freud, 1912b) to the clinical material is central to the functioning of the therapist as a reliable data collection instrument. This capacity, an openness to attend without preconceived biases to virtually all that there is to observe in the client's presentation, also includes his "receptive awareness" (D. J. Siegel, 2007) to be simultaneously open to his own unconscious responses to the clinical material. This twofold thrust of the therapist's intersubjective awareness of the two selves in the relationship dyad is a byproduct of his intense clinical concentration on affect states, physical sensations, body postures, facial displays, and intuitions as they reverberate within his own unconscious system. This state of mindfulness (Epstein, 2007) defines the clinician's stance of an "evenly suspended attention" as the characteristic feature of the clinician's attentional set, and once developed, activated, and maintained over time becomes what D. J. Siegel (2007) has described as an "intention to attend." From "effortful control" of his evenly suspended attentional stance, a stable and enduring, ever-shifting and mobile awareness of self and client emerges as a characteristic therapeutic state that informs practice. This stable state of attention to variously concentrate on the inner experience of the self as therapist in interaction with the client as object, with exercise and practice over time, can become an enduring character trait of the "effortless mindfulness" (D. J. Siegel, 2007) that defines one's professional identity and one's orientation as a psychotherapist. This stable state of clinical attention, the mindful awareness of self and other, is the defining dynamic of a depth-oriented and psychodynamically informed perspective on the multiple processes operating simultaneously in the therapy dyad. Developing this state of awareness, this effortful therapeutic control goes to the very core of the supervisory experience of intense concentration on all aspects of the clinical interview. The focus on stable states of attention and the effortful control of awareness of the therapeutic self defines a clinical supervision committed to the ongoing development of the mindfulness of the practitioner. Speculatively, the neurobiology implications of this clinicianly focus on self-awareness, mindfulness, and a prevailing attitude of "evenly suspended attention" suggest an enrichment of cerebral cellular mass in the neural circuits in the right hemisphere from repeated synaptic firings in the neocortex and limbic systems. Indeed, research findings from studies of subjects experienced in Zen meditation have demonstrated this plausible relationship between the practice of mindful awareness and the growth of the mentalizing structures located in the cerebral right hemisphere. This capacity for clinical concentration, commencing as a stable state of attention, matures over time and, with further refinement, through clinical supervision and self-reflection, changes from a stable trait to an enduring character trait of mindfulness—intrapsychically as a synthetic function of the ego, interpersonally as a foundation for intersubjective practice, phenomenologically as a forum for the exchange of affects, and neurobiologically as "what fires together, wires together" (Hebb, 1949, p. 70) further enhances the resonance and attachment circuits of the brain.

From the clinical internships in practice settings preparatory to attaining advanced graduate and professional school degrees to the myriad experiences of consultations with seasoned experts, the focus on clinicianly self-awareness, transference and countertransference phenomena, and all aspects of self-aware practice through intensive supervision initiates "harnessing the hub" (D. J. Siegel, 2007, p. 125). Conceptualized as a "wheel of awareness," the executive hub at the center of the wheel directs the clinician's attention to its rim as he concentrates his attention, via the spokes, to the rim of the wheel and pinpoints the salient clinical phenomena at hand.

The wheel of awareness depicted in Siegel's model of mindfulness provides a spatial display, as do all models that purport to represent theoretical structures, of the relationship between the executive hub, the spokes that connect the hub in the center to the rim on the outer periphery, that is, the boundary between internal experience and the outer environment, and the four sectors on the surface of the rim itself. As a dynamic metaphor for the mindfulness, nonjudgmental attitude, and evenly suspended attention, and all of the aspects of awareness that define the clinician's informed inquiry into therapeutic process, the wheel of awareness provides for a self and other focus for whatever is clinically significant at any given point in time. The focus of attention can be alternately directed toward self experience, client experience, or toward the interchange occurring within the therapy dyad itself.

The first sector of the rim enables clinicians to focus on the world outside, the non-self domain as it is perceived by any of the first five senses of sight, sound, taste, touch, and smell that sample the external environment. An example would be the clinician's first awareness of the client's nose or ear stud that now complements his body self or the orange, blue, and blond hair tints that now boldly enshrine her face. Of course, the clinical significance of these sensory impressions would vary considerably, prompting further reflection and dialogue and possibly serving as an entry into meaningful material, or not, as the case may be.

The second sector of the rim involves the bodily sensations in the interior—what is visceral, hormonal, and sensorimotor—the processes of interoception that may give rise to an intuitive hunch as the tensions of the musculature, for instance in the face or abdomen or a rise in respiratory rate set off neural net processes in the brain stem that inform the clinician emotionally. This sector of the rim correlates with Siegel's sixth sense.

The third and fourth sectors on the rim of the wheel of awareness represent the constructions that inform clinical practice in the mentalizing and relational dimensions of mindsightedness and attunement. The seventh sense includes all attentional engagements relating to experiences of self with other in the realms of emotion, attitude, perception, cognition, and whatever else that has psychological significance, for example, dreams and memories, that enable the clinician to gain insight through mindful awareness and to deepen his empathic resonance with the client. The most noteworthy feature of this "aim and sustain" focus of clinical attention in the treatment dyad is an awareness of being aware and an ability to think about thinking in mentalizing clinical phenomena. In the relational eighth sense, clinicians step into the life space of their adolescent clients and join them, empathically through vicarious introspection as they both witness and resonate with their clients' lived, felt, encoded, and represented interpersonal experiences. In sum, these sixth, seventh, and eighth senses that correspond to the second, third, and fourth sectors on the rim of the wheel become the foci of attention that ground the therapy in its conscious elements as well as at the nonconceptual level of implicit relational knowing.

Departing from "top down" vertical processing modes that are linear, language-based, logical, and left hemispheric, clinicians become increasingly facile in the tacit realm of nonconceptual, implicit relational knowing. For Epstein (2007) this mindfulness—exercising a therapeutic reflective awareness consonant with Freud's recommendation for maintaining an evenly suspended attention to all facets of the clinical situation—is a synthetic function of the ego, equal in significance to the role of the ego in its mastery of the drives, its regulation of the self system and its self representations, its defensive function, and in its adaptation to the external environment. In its synthetic function, this effortless mindfulness of the therapist, as both a reliable character trait and as an organizer of subjective data, permits the clinician to enter an interpersonal field of affective experiencing wherein he attunes, with empathy, to the feelings of his adolescent client. These two subjective affective cores, once bridged, return the adolescent client to his early attachment narrative and to the representations of his developmental history in the first separation-individuation stage.

The neurobiological underpinnings of therapeutic self-reflection, and the deployment of empathic communications that resonate with the client's affect states, correspond to neural processes that are located in the cerebral right hemisphere. It is in the medial pre-frontal region and in the anterior cingulate cortex where implicit memories and emotion are represented (Cozolino, 2002; D. J. Siegel, 2007). These "resonance circuits" of attunement with linkages via the insula serve to integrate the neocortex, the mirror neuron and limbic systems, physiological processes (visceral sensations, heart rate, and respiration), and the social worlds of the minds of self and others. The mindful awareness of the therapist as an observing self, an experiencing self, and as an attuning self to the relationship with his adolescent client operationalizes empathic therapeutic communication through the joining of these right hemispheric structures and their vertical circuitries. Through the activation of the mirror neuron system the therapist engages in a knowing of the emotions in his adolescent client. The perception of these affects, empathically understood and communicated, deepens the treatment relationship with the adolescent and promotes the further growth and maturation of these same cerebral structures and neural circuits responsible for affect regulation and reflective awareness: the mindsight capacities for insight, foresight, and hindsight. These capacities are located in the right hemisphere and specifically in the prefrontal, medial, and anterior cingulate cerebral neocortex, all of which are undergoing profound reorganization and change throughout the entire adolescent phase of development.

The internal validity of a procedure, that is, the confidence that the measurement of outcomes is based on the relationship predicated in the alternative hypothesis, relies on three interrelated aspects of rules of correspondence. The first is the adequacy of translation from the conceptual definitions of the variables under study to their operational equivalents. The second would be the accuracy and constancy of the measurement process itself, including the reliability residing within the human instrument who perceives, then processes, and finally translates one more time between the world of abstraction and the physical domain. Lastly is the sufficiency of situational controls to permit heightened systematic variance by keeping error variance at a minimum, that is, the minimax principle (Kerlinger, 1973). It is in the second and third of these that the intensive case study of psychotherapeutic process surpasses other methodologies in achieving the rigor necessary for a determination of internal validity.

In the therapeutic domain, the person of the practitioner—the trained professional self and all of its manifestations thereof—remains constant. This stability, therefore, permits the clinician's technical activity (the independent variable) to be free to vary as the underlying inert aspects of his personality—capacity for accurate empathy, experience, self-awareness, and confidence—stay the same. Thus, for example, if interpretation within the metaphor is conceptualized as the antecedent variable to be operationalized in the clinical activity with an adolescent, then its refinement and consistency within the professional using it lend impressive weight to the argument for reliability when its effects are later measured. Due to the practitioner's considerable potential for knowledge of his subject, vertically, as well as across situations, he is in a unique position to be aware of significant changes in the client's life space that could concomitantly affect progress in treatment. Of course, assigning weight to one or another of environmental versus therapeutic events would be admittedly no easy task; yet the practitioner himself, trained to be constant, objective, and self-aware above all, is better equipped than most other instruments to perform this monitoring function.

In this respect, then, the clinician-researcher engages in an enterprise that eschews a simplistic demonstration of the reversibility of client behaviors following the presence and absence of superficial, behaviorist interventions. Furthermore, the inherent complexity of the ecology of therapy (Heineman-Pieper, 1985) is fully recognized; and instead of isolating client behaviors that exclude the vast majority of the personality and characteristics of the client, an intense bipersonal field is highlighted so that multiple variables can be viewed and understood in their correlation to one another rather than as unitary causes that precede univariate effects. Rendering such a full recognition of the acuity and astuteness of clinical judgment amounts to a controlling and factoring in of variables rather than a controlling out of "extraneous" elements that is so notably a goal of single organism research strategy (Wodarski & Bagarozzi, 1979). Finally, such an ecosystem perspective inherent to rigorous case study methodology guards against a myopic explanatory theory, for example, that by specifying the reinforcement schedule in the token economy treatment contract, there has been no loss of information about the larger psychology of *Homo sapiens*. Guarded against as well is reductionism, that is, that a few universal laws can justifiably absorb carefully delimited and circumspect, but less grandiose, microtheory.

The mindfulness model of therapeutic process in the mentalizing psychotherapies with Jim in chapter 2 and with Karla and Fred in chapter 3 operationalized the clinician's contribution to the therapy relationship through a pervasive orientation of an "evenly suspended attention." This multifaceted orientation to be open to an awareness of all that transpires in the treatment relationship was an organismic variable that elicited significant data in Jim's attachment to me as a self object. My reflecting on his affect states, especially his frustration in relationship to the mother of separation, were the outcomes of the attunements I performed as an idealized selfobject. These empathic communications were all predicated on my implicit awareness of the meanings underlying his facial displays, tone of voice, and body postures. My evenly suspended attention to these nonverbal expressions of negativism and anger informed my soothing function role as I quietly empathized with his emotional distress in emancipating from her and her internalized presence as a maternal representation of an all-controlling bad object. Sharing my mentalized version of her with Jim enabled him to eventually reflect on her infantilizing control of him as a manifestation of her own ambivalence over his developing capacities for autonomy and independent functioning. My mindful awareness and open receptivity in Jim's treatment to his separation conflicts informed all aspects of the therapy, including the basis for verbal communication and empathy; the reconstruction of his separation anxieties vis-à-vis other adolescent patients with whom he shared similarities as well as notable differences in psychodynamics; my working model of Jim as well as the working models of the minds of his parents; my autonoetic time travel to the past to revisit my own separation narrative; and the reflective functions attendant to regulating my affects in my countertransference reactions to both Jim and his parents. From my mindful awareness of the vicissitudes in the dyad and effortful control of the focus on the three subjectivities involved in the treatment relationship—the patient's, the therapist's, and their shared intersubjective co-creation in between—the research data emerged for analysis, review, synthesis, and interpretation as specimens of subjectively informed, qualitative clinical inquiry.

At the center of the wheel of awareness, the executive hub functions to organize the focus of attention and direct it, via the spokes, to the eight sectors on the rim. Those sectors of the rim most involved in the cases of Jim, Karla, and Fred correspond to the visceral sixth sense, the mentalizing seventh sense, and the relational attunement eighth sense. It was with a heightened sense of internal tension, agitation, and increased heart rate and respiration that I experienced Jim's selfobject merger transference with me, especially in the performance of the explicit pretend roles in the Dungeons and Dragons game. These visceral clues prompted my intuitive sense that their source was an internalized and disavowed alien self as a son in interaction with an internalized and disapproving paternal object representation. These reflections pointed to the affects of humiliation and shame that pervaded so many of Jim's interpersonal experiences with family members and peers and to the underlying, compensatory grandiose self that served as his defense. In a similar vein, my reflective focus on Karla's immersion in the lives of her peers and her separation conflicts with her mother as a symbiotic object were therapeutic activities that operationalized a mindsight-oriented approach to understanding self, other, and interpersonal experience. This subjective clinical data confirmed her early separation arrest history and informed the treatment with details of her narrative that could have been retrieved in no other possible way.

Earlier in this chapter I outlined the five dimensions for assessing the validity of a qualitative case analysis of psychotherapy process. It is the consumers of such case reports who will ultimately determine whether or not the theoretical constructs correspond to the data collected and decide if the demonstrated relationships between the variables are of sufficient strength to warrant the retention of the alternative hypothesis. Because case studies are so sensitive to cultural surrounds, clients are contextualized in the myriad influences afforded by race, ethnicity, socioeconomic status, systems of belief, and all of the influences that derive from the environment and one's heritage. The extent to which the case report includes a narrative of these contextual and cultural influences is another measure of its adequacy as a qualitative research product. Finally, if the case study includes a review of the treatment as a process, then the reflexivity of the account itself, where the therapist as subject immerses himself explicitly in the dynamic interchanges within the dyad and simultaneously retrieves himself as an object for reflection and analysis, provides another guideline for assessing the validity of the psychotherapy narrative.

The dynamics of a second separation-individuation highlighted the treatment relationship in each of the therapies described in chapters 2, 3, and 4, and the case presentations of Jeff and Jennifer featured how their own unique cultural influences—Jeff's Scottish heritage as a warrior and Jennifer's rural eastern European ancestry—wrapped around their emergent identities as key metaphoric elements in their dream work as an Army Ranger/highlander and a ballerina/rhinoceros. These mythic images and their multiple affective meanings, both manifest and latent, inured the therapies with a perspective on their current developmental adolescent stage with derivatives from their distant but unique cultural pasts. This aspect of qualitative clinical validation, the pervasiveness of descriptive details of a mythic, familial heritage that grounds the adolescent in a storied narration through the generations, addresses the relevance of the study and its overall credibility (Mays & Pope, 1996). That my two dreams represented lingering "day residues" of clinical process with each of these adolescent clients, as countertransference manifestations as well as being thematic of my own ongoing process of identity consolidation, speaks to the reflexivity dimension of case study evaluation.

These above strengths inherent in a soundly conceptualized case study argue in favor of drawing an inference of an effect (outcome) when it has actually occurred by manipulating controlled events (type of treatment). In fact, the typical group experiment is woefully weak in this regard. The usual statistical tests for the significance of difference between means in the control and experimental conditions at times 0, X, and 0 rely upon average scores across a sufficiently large N. The effects of treatment, therefore, are never understood on a subject-by-subject basis. And most significantly, who changes, how much, when, and with what intensity of fluctuation is usually lost to the leavening effect of a statistical average (Leitenberg, 1973). In a dread worst-instance scenario, a type two error is made that erroneously asserts the truth of the null, ignoring real gains in the treated group when they have actually transpired. The above would be most likely to occur when the measurements of outcome were unreliable, invalid, or both, all of which emerge as less frequent problems in the case-intensive methodology proposed here. Finally, the intensive analysis of client change, as a process over time with many measurements rather than only two, is a powerful method that is potentiated when a time series feature is added to the monitoring of client movement in treatment.

Summary

At the heart of any scientific discipline are the elements of its theoretical structure, the reliable and valid classification of procedures and conditions: diagnostics, assessments, interventions, and processes. Social work in the clinical realm is currently striving for such an accurate specification of its basic concepts relative to treatment of the person in situation. The building blocks of theory are its constructs and to the end of knowledge refinement, paradigms are mobilized to aid in this endeavor, purified and modified, and then eventually discarded when no longer needed. Constructs are thus only relative in their importance to theory development and enjoy but a brief breath of life before becoming significant history.

It has been proposed elsewhere (Finestone & Kahn, 1975) that the intensive case study approach would be best utilized when knowledge in a given area is least developed and that experimental procedures should be reserved for the ultimate test of theory in the laboratory only after variables' effects in the field have been fully studied and elaborated. Such a view rigidly compromises the evolution and enhancement of clinical theory. It also foists upon the research enterprise a false dichotomy between laboratory and field, pragmatism-empiricism and an evolved philosophy of science, objectivity and subjectivity, and between quantitative measurement and informed qualitative clinical judgments.

As an aid in the conceptualizing of clinical assessment and the effects of treatment, the case study introduces practitioners to key elements of the profession's knowledge base and highlights, as well, its professional code of ethics. Every case study provides a cogent point of entry into the realm of the ethical and the ideal professional use of self. In summary, developmental theory and clinical practice find a natural and dramatic intersection as the client and therapist leap off the page in the intensive case study review of what the clinician thought and did and how the client responded. Most clinicians have a desire for such knowledge, and case study methodology is a better vehicle than most for exemplifying it.

It has been suggested in this concluding chapter that certain important continuities exist between the logic of the pure laboratory experiment and the pursuit of clinical knowledge through intensive case study analyses. These continuities inhere in the certainty that comes from control of the problem to be studied, control of the case which samples a population, control of the treatment domain, and reliable and valid control of the procedures operationalized. The intensive case study, ideally suited to professional practice ethically, in its pragmatics, and with its scientific rigor, can undoubtedly serve the clinical goals of theory development, variable refinement, and hypothesis testing, leading ultimately to construct validation. Its potential in these regards has yet to be tapped.

References

Allen, J. G., Fonagy, P., & Bateman, M. A. (2008). *Mentalizing in clinical practice*. Washington, DC: American Psychiatric Publishing.

American Psychiatric Association. (2000). *Diagnostic and statistical manual of mental disorders* (4th ed., text revision). Washington, DC: American Psychiatric Association.

Aronfreed, J. (1970). The socialization of altruistic and sympathetic behavior: Some theoretical and experimental analyses. In J. Macaulay & L. Berkowitz (Eds.), *Altruism and helping behavior*. New York: Academic Press.

Atwood, G., & Stolorow, R. (1999). *Faces in a cloud: Intersubjectivity in personality theory.* Northvale: Aronson.

Atwood, G., Stolorow, R., & Trop, J. (1989). *Impasses in psychoanalytic psychotherapy: A royal road.* New York: William Alanson White Institute.

Balint, M. (1968). *The basic fault: Therapeutic aspects of regression.* New York: Brunner/Mazel.

Barton, B. R., & Martin-Days, C. (1982). Adolescent depression: Significant issues in the diagnosis and treatment of constricted adolescents. *Clinical Social Work Journal, 10,* 275–288.

Basch, M. F. (1980). *Doing psychotherapy.* New York: Basic Books.

Becker, J. V., & Kavoussi, R. J. (1988). Sexual disorders. In J. Talbot, R. Hales, and S. Yudofsky (Eds.), *Textbook of psychiatry* (pp. 587–603). Washington, DC: American Psychiatric Press.

Beebe, B., & Lachman, F. M. (1988). Mother-infant mutual influence and precursors of psychic structure. In A. Goldberg (Ed.), *Progress in self psychology* (Vol. 3, pp. 3–25). Hillsdale, NJ: Analytic Press.

Blanck, G., & Blanck, R. (1974). *Ego psychology: Theory and practice.* New York: Columbia University Press.

Blanck, G., & Blanck, R. (1986). *Beyond ego psychology: Developmental object relations theory.* New York: Columbia University Press.

Blos, P. (1962). *On adolescence: A psychoanalytic interpretation.* New York: Free Press of Glencoe.

Blos, P. (1965). The initial stage of male adolescence. *Psychoanalytic Study of the Child, 20,* 145–164.

Blos, P. (1967). The second individuation process of adolescence. *Psychoanalytic Study of the Child, 22,* 162–186.

Blos, P. (1968). Character formation in adolescence. *Psychoanalytic Study of the Child, 23,* 245–263.

Blos, P. (1970). *The young adolescent: Clinical studies.* New York: Free Press.

Blos, P. (1972). The function of the ego ideal in adolescence. *Psychoanalytic Study of the Child, 27,* 93–97.

Blos, P. (1974). The genealogy of the ego ideal. *Psychoanalytic Study of the Child, 29,* 43–88.

Blos, P. (1985). *Son and father: Before and beyond the oedipal complex.* New York: Free Press.

Bowlby, J. (1969). *Attachment and loss: Vol. 1, Attachment.* New York: Free Press.

Boyer, L. B. (1983). *The regressed patient.* New York: Aronson.

Brandell, J. R. (2004). *Psychodynamic social work.* New York: Columbia University Press.

Brown, D. (1993). Affect development, psychopathology, and adaptation. In S. Ablon, D. Brown, E. Khantzian, & J. Mack (Eds.), *Human feelings: Explorations in affect development and meaning* (pp. 5–66). Hillsdale, NJ: Analytic Press.

Brown, L. M., & Gilligan, C. (1992). *Meeting at the crossroads.* New York: Ballatine.

Bruner, J. (1986). *Actual minds, possible worlds.* Cambridge, MA: Harvard University Press.

Burston, D. (1986). The cognitive and dynamic unconscious. *Comparative Psychoanalysis, 22*(1), 133–157.

Campbell, D. T., & Stanley, J. C. (1963). *Experimental and quasi-experimental designs for research.* Chicago: Rand McNally.

Chodorow, N. (1989). *Feminism and psychoanalytic theory.* New Haven, CT: Yale University Press.

Cook, T. D., & Campbell, D. T. (1979). *Quasi-experimentation: Design and analysis issues for field settings.* Chicago: Rand McNally.

Coppolillo, H. P. (1980). The tides of change in adolescence. In S. I. Greenspan & G. H. Pollock (Eds.), *The course of life: Psychoanalytic contributions toward understanding personality development, Vol. 2: Latency, adolescence, and youth.* Washington, DC: U.S. Department of Health and Human Services.

Cozolino, L. J. (2002). *The neuroscience of psychotherapy.* New York: W. W. Norton.

Edelson, J. L. (1978). A Piagetian approach to social work practice with children and adolescents. *Clinical Social Work Journal, 6*(1), 3–15.

Edwards, J. (1976). The therapist as a catalyst in promoting separation individuation. *Clinical Social Work Journal, 4*(3), 172–186.

Ekstein, R. (1966). *Children of time and space, of action and impulse.* New York: Meredith.

Emde, R. N. (1980). Toward a psychoanalytic theory of affect, II. Emerging models of emotional development in infancy. In S. I. Greenspan & G. H. Pollock (Eds.), *The course of life: Psychoanalytic contributions toward understanding personality development, Vol. 1: Infancy and early childhood* (pp. 85–112). Washington, DC: U.S. Department of Health and Human Services.

Epstein, M. (2007). Attention in analysis (chapter 5). *Psychotherapy without the self: A Buddhist perspective.* New Haven, CT: Yale University Press.

Erikson, E. H. (1959). Identity and the life cycle. *Selected papers, vol. 1.* New York: International Universities Press.

Erikson, E. H. (1963). *Childhood and society.* New York: W. W. Norton.

Erikson, E. H. (1968). Theoretical interlude (chapter 5). *Identity: Youth and crisis.* New York: W. W. Norton.

Finestone, S., & Kahn, A. J. (1975). The design of research. In N. A. Polansky (Ed.), *Social work research.* Chicago: University of Chicago Press.

Fonagy, P., Gergely, G., Jurist, E., & Target, M. (2002). *Affect regulation, mentalization, and the development of the self.* New York: W. W. Norton.

Fossage, J. (1998). Self psychology and its contributions to psychoanalysis. *Psychoanalytic Social Work, 5*(2), 1–18.

Fraiberg, S. (1981). The muse in the kitchen: A case study in clinical research. In H. Weschler et al. (Eds.), *Social work research in the human services.* New York: Human Sciences.

Freud, A. (1946). *The ego and the mechanisms of defence*. New York: International Universities Press.

Freud, S. (1900). The interpretation of dreams. In *The standard edition of the complete psychological works of Sigmund Freud* (Vols. 4 and 5, pp. 1–627). London: Hogarth.

Freud, S. (1905a). Fragment of an analysis of a case of hysteria. In *The standard edition of the complete psychological works of Sigmund Freud* (Vol. 7, pp. 1–122). London: Hogarth.

Freud, S. (1905b). Three essays on the theory of sexuality. In *The standard edition of the complete psychological works of Sigmund Freud* (Vol. 7, pp. 3–243 of chapter 1). London: Hogarth.

Freud, S. (1909a). Analysis of a phobia in a five year old boy. In *The standard edition of the complete psychological works of Sigmund Freud* (Vol. 10, pp. 1–149). London: Hogarth.

Freud, S. (1909b). Family romances. In *The standard edition of the complete psychological works of Sigmund Freud* (Vol. 9). London: Hogarth.

Freud, S. (1911a). Formulations on the two principles of mental functioning. In *The standard edition of the complete psychological works of Sigmund Freud* (Vol. 12, pp. 3–182). London: Hogarth.

Freud, S. (1911b). Psycho-analytical notes upon an autobiographical account of a case of paranoia. In *The standard edition of the complete psychological works of Sigmund Freud* (Vol. 12, pp. 1–82). London: Hogarth.

Freud, S. (1912a). The dynamics of transference. In *The standard edition of the complete psychological works of Sigmund Freud* (Vol. 12, pp. 97–108). London: Hogarth.

Freud, S. (1912b). Recommendations to physicians practising psycho-analysis. In *The standard edition of the complete psychological works of Sigmund Freud* (Vol. 20, pp. 75–125). London: Hogarth.

Freud, S. (1913). The disposition to obsessional neurosis. In *The standard edition of the complete psychological works of Sigmund Freud* (Vol. 12, pp. 313–316). London: Hogarth.

Freud, S. (1914). On narcissism. In *The standard edition of the complete psychological works of Sigmund Freud* (Vol. 14, pp. 67–102). London: Hogarth.

Freud, S. (1915a). A case of paranoia running counter to the psychoanalytical theory of the disease. In *The standard edition of the complete psychological works of Sigmund Freud* (Vol. 14). London: Hogarth.

Freud, S. (1915b). Repression. In *The standard edition of the complete psychological works of Sigmund Freud* (Vol. 14, pp. 143–158). London: Hogarth.

Freud, S. (1915c). The unconscious. In *The standard edition of the complete psychological works of Sigmund Freud* (Vol. 14, pp. 159–215). London: Hogarth.

Freud, S. (1917). Mourning and melancholia. In *The standard edition of the complete psychological works of Sigmund Freud* (Vol. 14, pp. 237–258). London: Hogarth.

Freud, S. (1920). Beyond the pleasure principle. In *The standard edition of the complete psychological works of Sigmund Freud* (Vol. 18, pp. 4–67). London: Hogarth.

Freud, S. (1923). The ego and the id. In *The standard edition of the complete psychological works of Sigmund Freud* (Vol. 19, pp. 3–59). London: Hogarth.

Freud, S. (1924). The dissolution of the Oedipus complex. In *The standard edition of the complete psychological works of Sigmund Freud* (Vol. 19, pp. 173–179). London: Hogarth.

Freud, S. (1926). Inhibitions, symptoms, and anxiety. In *The standard edition of the complete psychological works of Sigmund Freud* (Vol. 23, pp. 75–175). London: Hogarth.

Freud, S. (1931). Libidinal types. In *The standard edition of the complete psychological works of Sigmund Freud* (Vol. 21, pp. 215–220). London: Hogarth.

Freud, S. (1940). Splitting of the ego in the process of defence. In *The standard edition of the complete psychological works of Sigmund Freud* (Vol. 23, pp. 271–278). London: Hogarth.

Frieswyk, S. H., Allen, J. G., Colson, D. B., Coyne, L., Gabbard, G. O., Horwitz, L., & Newsom, G. (1986). The therapeutic alliance: Its place as a process and outcome variable in psychotherapy research. *Journal of Consulting and Clinical Psychology, 54*, 32–38.

Gabbard, G. O. (2005). *Psychodynamic psychiatry in clinical practice*. Washington, DC: American Psychiatric Publishing.

Gallese, V. C., Keysers, C., & Rizzolatti, G. (2004). A unifying view of the basis of social cognition. *Trends in Cognitive Sciences, 8*(9), 396–403.

Gedo, J., & Goldberg, A. (1973). *Models of the mind*. Chicago: University of Chicago Press.

Geertz, C. (1973). *The interpretation of cultures.* New York: Basic Books.

Gilligan, C. (1982). New maps of development, new visions of maturity. *American Journal of Orthopsychiatry, 5*(2), 192–212.

Gilligan, C. (1993). *In a different voice.* Cambridge, MA: Harvard University Press.

Giovacchini, P. L. (1979). *Treatment of primitive mental states.* New York: Aronson.

Goldberg, A. (1978). *The psychology of the self: A casebook.* New York: International Universities Press.

Goldstein, M. J., & Palmer, J. O. (1978). *The experience of anxiety.* New York: Oxford University Press.

Greenacre, P. (1958). Early physical determinants in the sense of identity. *Emotional growth* (Vol. 1, 1971, pp. 113–127). New York: International Universities Press.

Greenacre, P. (1960). *Emotional growth, 1: Considerations regarding the parent-infant relationship.* New York: International Universities Press.

Greenspan, S. I., & Polk, W. G. (1980). A developmental approach to the assessment of adult personality functioning and psychopathology. In S. I. Greenspan & G. H. Pollock (Eds.). *The course of life: Psychoanalytic contributions toward understanding personality development, Vol. 3: Adulthood and the aging process* (pp. 255–297). Washington, DC: U.S. Department of Health and Human Services.

Grossbard, H. (1962). Ego deficiency in delinquents. *Social Casework, 43,* 172–178.

Gunderson, J. G., & Singer, M. T. (1975). Defining borderline patients: An overview. *American Journal of Psychiatry, 132,* 1–9.

Gutmann, D. L. (1980). Psychoanalysis and aging: A developmental view. In S. I. Greenspan & G. H. Pollock (Eds.), *The course of life: Psychoanalytic contributions toward understanding personality development, Vol. 3: Adulthood and the aging process.* Washington, DC: U.S. Department of Health and Human Services.

Harley, M. (1970). On some problems of techniques in the analysis of early adolescents. *Psychoanalytic Study of the Child, 17,* 42–81.

Harter, S. (1999). *The construction of the self.* New York: Guilford.

Harter, S., & Buddin, B. (1987). Children's understanding of the simultaneity of two emotions: A five-stage developmental acquisition sequence. *Developmental Psychology, 23*(3), 388–399.

Hartmann, H. (1939). *Ego psychology and the problem of adaptation.* New York: International Universities Press.

Hartmann, H., & Lowenstein, R. (1962). Notes on the superego. *Psychoanalytic Study of the Child, 17,* 42–81.

Hebb, D. O. (1949). *The organization of behavior: A neuropsychological theory.* New York: Wiley.

Heineman, M. B. (1981). The obsolete scientific imperative in social work research. *Social Services Review, 55,* 371–397.

Heineman-Pieper, M. (1985). The future of social work research. *Social Work Research and Abstracts, 21*(4), 3–11.

Horney, K. (1945). *Our inner conflicts: A constructive theory of neurosis.* New York: W. W. Norton.

Horvath, A. D., & Symonds, B. D. (1991). Relation between working alliance and outcome in psychotherapy: A meta-analysis. *Journal of Counseling Psychology, 38,* 139–149.

Howe, M. W. (1974). Casework self-evaluation: A single subject approach. *Social Service Review, 48,* 1–23.

Imre, R. (1982). *Knowing and caring: Philosophical issues in social work.* New York: University Press of America.

Jacobson, E. (1964). *The self and the object world.* New York: International Universities Press.

Jacobson, E. (1971). *Depression: Comparative studies of normal, neurotic and psychotic conditions.* New York: International Universities Press.

Jaques, E. (1980). The midlife crisis. In S. I. Greenspan & G. H. Pollock (Eds.), *The course of life: Psychoanalytic contributions toward understanding personality development, Vol. 3: Adulthood and the aging process* (1–23). Washington DC: U.S. Department of Health and Human Services.

Jayaratne, S. (1977). Single subject and group designs in treatment evaluation. *Social Work Research and Abstracts, 13*(3), 35–42.

Johnson, A. (1949). Sanctions for superego lacunae of adolescents. In K. R. Eissler (Ed.), *Searchlights on delinquency.* New York: International Universities Press.

Jordan, J. V. (Ed.). (1997). *Women's growth in diversity: More writings from the Stone Center.* New York: Guilford.

Jordan, J. V., Kaplan, A. G., Miller, J. B., Stives, I. P., & Surrey, J. L. (1991). *Women's growth in connection: Writings from the Stone Center.* New York: Guilford.

Josselyn, I. (1971). *Adolescence.* New York: Harper and Row.

Jung, C. G. (1961). *Memories, dreams, reflections*. A. Jaffe (Ed.), R. Winston and C. Winston (Trans). New York: Vintage.

Kaufmann, I., & Heims, L. (1959). The body image of the juvenile delinquent. *American Journal of Orthopsychiatry, 29,* 146–159.

Kerlinger, F. N. (1973). *Foundations of behavioral research.* New York: Holt, Rinehart, and Winston.

Kernberg, O. F. (1966). Structural derivatives of object relationships. *International Journal of Psycho-Analysis, 47,* 236–253.

Kernberg, O. F. (1967). Borderline personality organization. *Journal of the American Psychoanalytic Association, 15,* 641–685.

Kernberg, O. F. (1976). *Object relations theory and clinical psychoanalysis.* New York: Aronson.

Kernberg, O. F. (1980). *Internal world and external reality: Object relations theory applied.* New York: Aronson.

Kestenberg, J. S. (1980). Eleven, twelve and thirteen: Years of transition from the barrenness of childhood to the fertility of adolescence. In S. I. Greenspan & G. H. Pollock (Eds.), *The course of life: Psychoanalytic contributions toward understanding personality development, Vol. 2: Latency, adolescence, and youth* (pp. 229–264). Washington DC: U.S. Department of Health and Human Services.

Kirk, S. A., & Kolevzon, M. S. (1978). Teaching research methodology from Z to A. *Journal of Education for Social Work, 14*(1), 66–72.

Klein, M. (1932). *Contributions to psychoanalysis.* A. Strachey (Trans.). New York: W. W. Norton.

Klein, M. (1935). A contribution to the psychogenesis of manic-depressive states. In *Love, Guilt and Reparation: The Writings of Melanie Klein* (Vol. 1, pp. 262–289). London: Hogarth.

Knight, R. (1953). Borderline states. In R. Lowenstein (Ed.), *Drives, affect, behavior.* New York: International Universities Press.

Kohlberg, L. (1976). Moral stages and moralization: The cognitive-developmental approach. In T. Lickona (Ed.), *Moral development and behavior: Theory, research, and social issues.* New York: Holt, Rinehart, and Winston.

Kohut, H. (1971). *Analysis of the self.* New York: International Universities Press.

Krystal, H., & Krystal, A. D. (1994). Creativity and affect. In M. P. Shaw & M. A. Runco (Eds.), *Psychoanalysis and neuroscience in relationship to dreams and creativity* (pp. 185–212). Westport, CT: Ablex.

Lackoff, G. (1987). *Women, fire and dangerous things: What categories reveal about the mind*. Chicago: University of Chicago Press.

Lackoff, G. (1997). How unconscious metaphorical thought shapes dreams. In D. J. Stein (Ed.), *Cognitive science and the unconscious* (pp. 89–120). Washington, DC: American Psychiatric Press.

Lampl-de-Groot, J. (1962). Ego ideal and superego. *Psychoanalytic Study of the Child, 17*, 94–106.

Laufer, M. (1968). The body image, the function of masturbation, and adolescence: Problems of ownership of the body. *Psychoanalytic Study of the Child, 23*, 114–137.

Lawson, D. M., & Brossart, D. F. (2003). Link among therapist and parent relationship, the working alliance, and therapy outcome. *Psychotherapy Research, 13*, 383–394.

Leitenberg, H. (1973). The use of single-case methodology in psychotherapy research. *Journal of Abnormal Psychology, 82*, 87–101.

Levin, F. M. (1980). Metaphor, affect, and arousal: How interpretations might work. *Annual of Psychoanalysis, 8*, 231–245.

Lichtenberg, J. (1989). *Psychoanalysis and motivation*. Hillsdale, NJ: Analytic Press.

Linn, M. W., & Greenwald, S. R. (1974). Student attitude, knowledge, and skill related to research training. *Journal of Education for Social Work, 10*, 48–54.

Loewald, H. W. (1980a). On the therapeutic action of psychoanalysis. *Papers on psychoanalysis* (pp. 221–256). New Haven, CT: Yale University Press.

Loewald, H. W. (1980b). Superego and time. In *Papers on psychoanalysis* (pp. 43–52). New Haven, CT: Yale University Press.

Luborsky, L., et al. (1980). Predicting the outcome of psychotherapy: Findings of the Penn psychotherapy research project. *Archives of General Psychiatry, 37*, 471–481.

Lucente, R. L. (1986). Self-transcending and the adolescent ego ideal. *Child and Adolescent Social Work Journal, 3*, 161–76.

Lucente, R. L. (1987). N = 1: Intensive case study methodology reconsidered. *Journal of Teaching in Social Work, 1*(2), 49–64.

Lucente, R. L. (1994). The concept of developmental lines in marital therapy. *Journal of Analytic Social Work, 2*(2), 57–75.

Lucente, R. L. (1996). Sexual identity: Conflict and confusion in a male adolescent. *Child and Adolescent Social Work Journal, 13*(2), 97–114.

Lucente, R. L. (2008). Affectivity: Regulation, identity formation, and metaphorical thought. *Psychoanalytic Social Work, 15*(1), 1–27.

Lucente, R. L., & Mishne, J. M. (2010). Clinical social work with adolescents. In J. R. Brandell (Ed.), *Theory and practice in clinical social work* (2nd ed., pp. 123–153). Thousand Oaks, CA: Sage.

Lyons-Ruth, K. (1999). Two-person unconscious: Intersubjective dialogue, enactive relational representation, and the emergence of new forms of relational organization. *Psychoanalytic Inquiry, 19*, 576–617.

MacKenzie, F. (2007). *Theory and practice with adolescents.* Chicago: Lyceum Books.

Mahler, M., Pine, F., & Bergman, A. (1975). *The psychological birth of the human infant.* New York: Basic Books.

Main, M., & Solomon, J. (1986). Discovery of an insecure disorganized/disoriented attachment pattern. In T. B. Brazelton & M. Yogman (Eds.), *Affective development in infancy* (pp. 95–124). Norwood: Ablex.

Martin, D. J., Garske, J. P., & Davis, M. K. (2000). Relation of the therapeutic alliance with outcome and other variables: A meta-analytic review. *Journal of Consulting and Clinical Psychology, 68*, 438–450.

Marziali, E., Marmar, C., & Krupnick, J. (1981). Therapeutic alliance scales: Development and relationship to psychotherapy outcome. *American Journal of Psychiatry, 138*, 361–364.

Masterson, J. F. (1972). *Treatment of the borderline adolescent: A developmental approach.* New York: Wiley and Sons.

Mays, N., & Pope, C. (1996). *Rigour in qualitative research.* London: BMJ Books.

Meeks, J. E., & Bernet, W. (2001). *The fragile alliance* (5th ed.). New York: Krieger.

Mischler, E. G. (1986). Meaning in context: Is there any other kind? *Harvard Educational Review, 49*(1), 1–19.

Mishne, J. M. (1986). *Clinical work with adolescents.* New York: Free Press.

Money, J. (1974). Intersexual and transexual behavior and syndromes. In S. Arieti (Ed.), *American handbook of psychiatry* (2nd ed., pp. 334–351). New York: Basic Books.

Mullen, E. J. (1985). Methodological dilemmas in social work research. *Social Work Research and Abstracts, 21*(4), 12–20.

Murphy, L. B., & Hirschberg, J. C. (1982). *Robin: Comprehensive treatment of a vulnerable adolescent.* New York: Basic Books.

Nass, M. L. (1966). The superego and moral development in the theories of Freud and Piaget. *Psychoanalytic Study of the Child, 21,* 51–68.

Novey, S. (1955). The role of the superego and ego-ideal in the character formation. *International Journal of Psychoanalysis, 36,* 254–259.

Ogden, T. H. (1994). The analytic third: Working with intersubjective clinical facts. *International Journal of Psychoanalysis, 75,* 3–19.

Palombo, J. (1987). Spontaneous self-disclosures in psychotherapy. *Clinical Social Work Journal, 15*(2), 107–120.

Palombo, J., & Feigon, J. (1984). Borderline personality development in childhood and its relationship to neurocognitive deficits. *Child and Adolescent Social Work Journal, 1*(1), 18–33.

PDM Task Force. (2006). *Psychodynamic diagnostic manual.* Silver Spring, MD: Alliance of Psychoanalytic Organizations.

Piaget, J. (1950). *The Psychology of intelligence.* London: Routledge and Kegan Paul and Humanities Press.

Piaget, J. (1965). *The moral judgment of the child.* New York: Free Press.

Piers, G., & Singer, M. (1971). *Shame and guilt.* New York: W. W. Norton.

Polanyi, M. (1962). *Personal knowledge.* Chicago: University of Chicago Press.

Polanyi, M. (1966). *The tacit dimension.* Garden City, NY: Doubleday.

Polanyi, M., & Prosch, H. (1975). *Meaning.* Chicago: University of Chicago Press.

Pollack, W. B. (2000). *Real boys' voices.* New York: Random House.

Rapaport, D. (1951). The autonomy of the ego. *Bulletin of the Menninger Clinic, 15,* 113–123.

Rapaport, D. (1958). The theory of ego autonomy. *Bulletin of the Menninger Clinic, 22,* 13–35.

Reid, W. J. (1972). Target problems, time limits, task structure. *Journal of Education for Social Work, 8*(2), 58–68.

Reid, W. J., & Epstein, L. (1977). *Task centered practice.* New York: Columbia University Press.

Reiter, L. (1989). Sexual orientation, sexual identity, and the question of choice. *Clinical Social Work Journal, 17*(2), 138–150.

REM. (2004). Leaving New York. *Around the sun.* Burbank, CA: Warner Bros. Records.

Richmond, M. E. (1917). *Social diagnosis.* New York: Russell Sage Foundation.

Rorty, R. (1991). *Objectivity, relativism, and truth: Philosophical papers, Volume 1.* Cambridge, UK: Cambridge University Press.

Rose, G. J. (1980). *The power of form: A psychoanalytic approach to aesthetic form*. New York: International Universities Press.

Rose, G. J. (1996). *Necessary illusion: Art as witness*. New York: International Universities Press.

Russell, P. (1998). The role of paradox in the repetition compulsion. In J. G. Teicholz & D. Kriegman (Eds.), *Trauma, repetition, and affect regulation: The work of Paul Russell* (pp. 1–22). New York: Other Press.

Saleebey, D. (1979). The tension between research and practice: Assumptions of the experimental paradigm. *Clinical Social Work Journal, 7*(4), 267–284.

Sander, L. W. (1980). Investigation of the infant and its caregiving environment as a biological system. In S. I. Greenspan & G. H. Pollock (Eds.), *The course of life: Psychoanalytic contributions toward understanding personality development, Vol. I: Infancy and early childhood* (pp. 177–202). Washington, DC: U.S. Department of Health and Human Services.

Sander, L. W. (2002). Thinking differently: Principles of process in living systems and the specificity of being known. *Psychoanalytic Dialogues, 12*(1), 11–42.

Sandler, J., Holder, A., & Meers, D. (1963). The ego ideal and the ideal self. *Psychoanalytic Study of the Child, 28*, 139–158.

Schafer, R. (1967). Ideals, the ego ideal, and the ideal self. In R. R. Holt (Ed.), *Motives and thought*. New York: International Universities Press.

Schafer, R. (1968). *Aspects of internalization*. New York: International Universities Press.

Scher, M. (1990). Effect of gender role incongruities on men: Experience as clients in psychotherapy. *Psychotherapy, 27*, 322–326.

Schore, A. N. (1994). *Affect regulation and the origin of the self: The neurobiology of emotional development*. Hillsdale, NJ: Erlbaum.

Schore, A. N. (2003). *Affect regulation and the repair of the self*. New York: W. W. Norton.

Selman, R. L. (1971). The relation of role taking to the development of moral judgments in children. *Child Development, 42*, 79–91.

Shakespeare, W. (1997). Othello. In *The Complete Works of William Shakespeare* (4th ed., pp. 1117–1166). D. Bevington (Ed.). New York: Addison-Wesley Educational.

Shopper, M. (1984). From re-discovery to ownership of the vagina: A contribution to the explanation of nonuse of contraceptives in the female adolescent. In M. Sugar (Ed.), *Adolescent Parenthood*. Jamaica: Spectrum.

Siegel, D. J. (1999). *The developing mind: How relationships and the brain inter-act to shape who we are.* New York: Guilford.

Siegel, D. J. (2007). *The mindful brain: Reflection and attunement in the cultiva-tion of well-being.* New York: W. W. Norton.

Siegel, J. P. (2007). The role of affect regulation in a case of attempted maternal-filicide suicide: Commentary on an act of despair. *Clinical Social Work Jour-nal, 35*(4), 223–228.

Spence, D. P. (1986). When interpretation masquerades as explanation. *Journal of the American Psychoanalytic Association, 34,* 3–22.

Spitz, R. (1965). *The first year of life.* New York: International Universities Press.

Staub, E. (1975). *The development of prosocial behavior in children.* New York: General Learning.

Stern, D. B. (1983). Unformulated experience: From familiar chaos to creative disorder. *Contemporary Psychoanalysis, 19*(1), 71–99.

Stern, D. N. (1985). *The interpersonal world of the infant.* New York: Basic Books.

Stoller, R. (1968). *Sex and gender: Vol. 1, The development of masculinity and femininity.* New York: Science House.

Strean, H. (1984). Psychosexual disorders. In F. J. Turner (Ed.), *Adult psycho-pathology: A social work perspective* (pp. 316–344). New York: Free Press.

Strupp, H. H. (1973). *Psychotherapy: Clinical, research, and theoretical issues.* New York: Aronson.

Sullivan, H. S. (1953). *The interpersonal theory of psychiatry.* New York: W. W. Norton.

Sullivan, T., & Schneider, M. (1987). Development and identity issues in adoles-cent homosexuality. *Child and Adolescent Social Work Journal, 4*(1), 13–24.

Thompson, R. A. (1994). Emotion regulation: A theme in search of definition. In N. A. Fox (Ed.), *Monographs of the Society for Research in Child Develop-ment, 59*(2–3), 25–52.

Tolpin, M. (1971). On the beginnings of a cohesive self: An application of the concept of transmuting internalization to the study of the transitional object and signal anxiety. *Psychoanalytic Study of the Child, 26,* 316–352.

Tomkins, S. (1962). *Affect, imagery, consciousness, Vol. 1, The positive affects.* New York: Springer.

Tomkins, S. (1963). *Affect, imagery, consciousness, Vol. 2, The negative affects.* New York: Springer.

Toolan, J. M. (1962). Depression in children and adolescents. *American Journal of Orthopsychiatry, 32,* 404–415.

Trevarthen, C. (1993). The self born in intersubjectivity: The psychology of infant communicating. In E. Neisser (Ed.), *The perceived self: Ecological and interpersonal sources of self-knowledge* (pp. 121–173). New York: Cambridge University Press.

Trevarthen, C. (1996). Lateral asymmetries in infancy: Implications for the development of the hemispheres. *Neuroscience and Biobehavioral Reviews, 20,* 571–586.

Wheeler, M. A., Stuss, D. T., & Tulving, F. (1997). Toward a theory of episodic memory: The frontal lobes and autonoetic consciousness. *Psychological Bulletin, 121*(3), 331–354.

White, R. W. (1959). Motivation reconsidered: The concept of competence. *Psychological Review, 66,* 297–333.

White, R. W. (1963). Ego and reality in psychoanalytic thought. *Psychological Issues, 3*(3), 1–210.

Winnicott, D. W. (1950). Aggression in relation to emotional development. In *Collected papers: Through pediatrics to psychoanalysis* (pp. 204–218). New York: Basic Books.

Winnicott, D. W. (1951). Transitional objects and transitional phenomena. In *Collected papers: Through pediatrics to psychoanalysis* (pp. 229–242). New York: Basic Books.

Winnicott, D. W. (1956). Primary maternal preoccupation. In *Collected papers: Through pediatrics to psychoanalysis* (pp. 300–315). New York: Basic Books.

Winnicott, D. W. (1958). The capacity to be alone. In *Collected papers: Through pediatrics to psychoanalysis* (pp. 29–36). New York: Basic Books.

Winnicott, D. W. (1960a). Ego distortion in terms of the true and false self. In *The maturational processes and the facilitating environment* (pp. 14–52). New York: International Universities Press.

Winnicott, D. W. (1960b). The theory of the parent-infant relationship. In *The maturational process and the facilitating environment* (pp. 37–55). New York: International Universities Press.

Winnicott, D. W. (1963). Communicating and not communicating leading to a study of certain opposites. In *The maturational process and the facilitating environment* (pp. 179–192). New York: International Universities Press.

Winnicott, D. W. (1967a). The location of cultural experience. In *Playing and reality* (pp. 95–103). New York: Basic Books.

Winnicott, D. W. (1967b). Mirror role of mother and family in child development. In *Playing and reality* (pp. 111–118). New York: Basic Books.

Wodarski, J. S., & Bagarozzi, D. A. (1979). A review of the empirical status of traditional modes of interpersonal helping: Implications for social work practice. *Clinical Social Work Journal, 7*(4), 231–255.

Zentner, M. (1984). Paranoia. In F. J. Turner (Ed.), *Adult psychopathology: A social work perspective* (pp. 364–383). New York: Free Press.

Zimbalist, S. (1977). *Historic themes and landmarks in social welfare research.* New York: Harper and Row.

Index

About the Author

Randolph L. Lucente (MSW, PhD, *Jane Addams College of Social Work, University of Illinois, Chicago*) is professor of social work at Loyola University Chicago and a former director of the doctoral program. He is a licensed clinical social worker and has a psychotherapy practice with adolescents, adults, and their families.